Dinner & Party

Dinner & Party

Gatherings. Suppers. Feasts.

ROSE PRINCE

SEVEN DIALS

CONTENTS

AN INVITATION TO DINNER & PARTY

'Come over.'

The simplest of all ways to issue an invite yet these two words mean one, some or all of the following: meet, eat, drink, share, celebrate and enjoy. It is an act of friendship and a unique human quality. No other being shares food outside the family to the extent that we do yet it is neither universal, in that everyone does it, nor is it instinctive, coming naturally to everyone. Even in a small way, cooking for friends is learned.

This is a book of practical recipes, ideal for entertaining. No matter your cooking ability, you will be able to put together a menu that is right for the occasion, your friends, the season and budget. Good hosts are often complimented for having made a meal look effortless which to me means more that the effort is hidden and consequently the gathering is enjoyably relaxed. Simple, clever ways of making the food look good, the right balance of flavours, sensible planning – these easy-to-adopt values underpin my Dinner & Party idea and are designed to inspire and be useful for both regular hosts and beginners. The litmus test for success is this: a party-giver should enjoy their day as much as their guests.

LIFE IS A PARTY

Some people grow up in homes where the door is always open to friends, and they take this custom into their own adulthood. For others, issuing that first invitation is momentous, a breakthrough into a pleasurable world but one that is not without challenges. Because in the simple, human act of inviting others into your home, you are revealing perhaps more about yourself than you might be at ease with: the inside of the sanctuary that is your household; your personal tastes in food and its presentation, your knowledge of what to drink with what and also – most dauntingly – your abilities.

It should not be so scary. Generally, the good manners of guests should give nothing but encouragement to their host – and gratitude. Socialising is about more than the prowess of the cook and yet we do seem to be living in an era of heightened analysis of food. Obsessive 'foodyism' brings a downside, putting off the beginner. When social media entitles everyone to assume the role of expert and critic, whether posting beautiful photographs of their own cooking or damning with their opinions the efforts of others when eating out, who dares to be an amateur? In this atmosphere the concept of simplicity is most at threat. Home cooks need to step back, be reminded that in the real world cooking for others at home is all about lightness of touch.

The cure for a shy host, someone who has not cooked often for friends let alone dared to ask a work colleague to dinner, is this: know a few recipes to begin with and practise them first if you can. Buy the best ingredients because it makes all the difference to flavour – shopping is 50 per cent of being a good cook – and always choose recipes you know are within your abilities and time schedule. Essentially, simplicity is immune to reproach.

DOING LESS

Do less – such a welcome thought and yet oddly hard to pull off at first. Natural generosity often leads to offering too much when a meal of simple ingredients, well chosen or sourced at the right time of year, leaves a much greater impression. I am not a critical guest. I care as much about being with people I love as I do the food, so am always happy to be asked anywhere. The only time I am irritated as a guest is when people do too much. Put it this way, meat and one veg is enough. I would rather someone focus on cooking a piece of meat well than have them dashing around buttering six vegetable dishes. If you only serve new potatoes, that is fine – in our kitchen we say that rocket with olive oil is a vegetable.

I do not say 'you cannot go wrong' lightly, but seasonal ingredients, especially locally sourced, cooked simply and presented with a drop of style, outrank every fussy meal ever offered. As an example, between April and late June, when English asparagus is in the shops, it is for me the only starter to serve either with extra virgin olive oil, butter or classic hollandaise. It is beautiful on its own without any decoration. Because British-grown asparagus is scarce for most of the rest of the year, to serve it adds an other essential element to the meal: a sense of occasion.

SOCIAL HISTORY – DO YOU REMEMBER WHEN?

This book of recipes for dinners and parties contains many memories going back as far as childhood. There are recipes from our family Christmases, barbecues and long summer lunches outdoors; winter picnics served out of the boot of the car, with Thermos and lukewarm sausages, celebration cakes. Some recipes are dishes from my first, oh-so-grown-up supper parties after leaving home, when the budget was tight and space round the kitchen table even more squeezed – I remember us sharing chairs and there being only enough cutlery to eat risotto with either a fork or spoon, but not both.

To discover you love to cook dinners for others opens up a new aspect to life for a young person finding their way, creating a reciprocal social pattern. Cook a good dinner and someone will think to ask you back. It is how I met many of my friends and, incidentally, my husband. This is particularly relevant now, when people are busier than ever and more widely scattered. Now that it is possible to maintain friendships via Facebook and the norm to find partners through digital dating sites, the traditional dinner or party held at home comes under threat. We need to make time for dinner, however. Getting around the table with half a dozen of your favourite people on a Friday night, throwing that open-ended bohemian drinks party for however many; planning that picnic-barbecue in the garden. These are the punctuation points; future stories – the do-you-remember-whens in life. Entertaining is a habit to keep even when progress is pulling at us to digitalise our social lives.

THE RITUALS OF DINNER

Sharing food has always been highly ritualised, from the laying of the table with favourite crockery, glass and cutlery; choosing linen, decorating with flowers, lighting candles, to the meal itself. Traditionally, this has been an ordered structure with appetisers and bread handed around, the spectacle of meat being carved at the table then the final reward of sweet puddings. While it is rare to opt for a three-course dinner, even a diluted form of these codes and customs connects to our respect for the sacred availability of food, the killing of our prey if you like.

We do like to toast in our home, raising glasses for all sorts of reasons. I think this has replaced the old custom of saying grace to give thanks for what is on the table.

Some say it's an affectation, but I think it is appropriate to mention if you are serving something remarkable, especially if your guests are as interested in food as you are. It might be locally reared meat from a special breed, something seasonal or handmade nearby – I do this as an acknowledgement, perhaps with silent gratitude and respect. Your passion for cooking and food itself will be infectious.

Saying please and thank you, not stretching to grab the butter, remembering not to stick your elbows into your neighbour while enthusiastically eating – there are many standards to remember in any food situation, and they vary from nation to nation. It is polite in Japan to make a slurping noise while eating soup and noodles. If you did that in Britain the whole room would fall silent, then stare. Scrunching up your napkin after eating is sign of appreciation in some countries, belching gives the same message in others. Elbows on the table, eating with your mouth open, yawning, using a toothpick – abhorrent in Britain and America but acceptable in most of Europe – what a minefield.

Meal rituals tend to be learned from parents. In our home, at a formal dinner, I was taught to serve from the left, clear from the right and always offer food first to the woman sitting on my father's right. I do not keep these rules at home, and usually plonk the serving dishes in the centre for people to help themselves, then noisily stack dishes at the table rather than take two at a time, discreetly placing one on top of the other, as I was taught. This is something of a rebellion.

I feel that manners are one thing, and mostly common sense, but rules belong in formal or professional situations. In a domestic setting such behaviour can have the effect of making some feel excluded. Meals need to be egalitarian, more about sharing food and less about keeping up. Snobbery in food culture is gradually, and thankfully, being undone. We can all eat dinner and party without it.

P.S. PARTYING WITHOUT COOKING

I know people who never cook, but who love to have people over to eat. I hope that they will try perhaps the simplest recipes in this book, or be inspired to persuade someone else to and enjoy replicating the style in its pages. I should not admit it but there are good imitations out there to buy. There is absolutely no shame in purchasing ready-made as long as you buy from a trusted source. In France, it has always been quite normal to buy dinner made by a traiteur or pudding from a patisserie. In fact, a host will boast to guests about the little shop that makes the excellent terrines on the table, or the mousses, soups, stuffed crêpes, fish gratins, meat braises and fruit tarts. In the absence of a good source of ready-made 'homemade', I suggest to people averse to cooking to devote their efforts to shopping and picnic indoors.

THE BASICS

Details do not all have to be learned at once. If you take one or two menus from this book and can cook them confidently that is fine. Dip in from time to time and build your range. This section, when you're ready, is all about the other elements of dinners and parties.

SPACE

Top of the list of excuses of why a person is afraid of entertaining at home is scale. 'My kitchen is too small'; 'my place is too tiny and four floors up . . .' If you commit to being flexible you can throw a party anywhere. Extinguish the outdated image of dinner parties only being held around a large table, piled with the family silver, a bowl of roses and snaking candelabra. Anything is possible and there is no written rule saying we must all eat at one table. Think out of the box in the literal sense. Small folding tables seat four and can be put up in different places, one in a corridor with others in the kitchen and/or living room. Splitting people into small groups actually creates an interesting social dynamic. Folding chairs are a help, too, and cheap to buy.

Obviously the size of a room or lack of outside space will restrict numbers, so give smaller parties more often. Stand-up parties in small spaces need one table for drinks and another for the kind of food people will gravitate towards to serve themselves, like the indoor picnic (page 218). It is stressful serving food in a cramped area, so avoid fork and plate food, and choose things that can be held in the hand with a napkin. Pans of soup or braises can be served straight from the hob, where they will anyway hold their heat. Tea trays (or laptop tables) with folding legs are useful for adding extra surface space on tables. I have seen the stairs in a small house used for drinks and glasses, and a tiny table set up inside a hallway coat cupboard as a makeshift bar. I was inspired by a friend who uses her ironing board, laid with a tablecloth, as a side table for serving food. In the garden, a wheelbarrow is a roomy ice bucket and mobile canteen. Outdoors you also need less furniture. Always have a few chairs for those who really need them, but cushions and rugs are fine for most – this feels very 'festival,' very laid-back.

Where a party happens often becomes the decision of the guests. We used to get two rooms ready for our winter party each year, hoping guests would disperse themselves tidily in both, but it never happened. Most wanted to be part of the crush in one room. Nor did our dinners ever mimic the seventies sophistication of my parents. My grown-up wish to have drinks in the living room, move to the kitchen table for dinner then out again to drink coffee, never happened. Guests would come straight into the kitchen and stay there, refusing to move.

I think everyone now sees the kitchen as a natural place to eat, precipitating a national movement to knock down walls between living and cooking areas. I hate the term 'kitchen supper', however. It is ridiculously snobbish. 'Dinner' says it all. When after twenty years we moved out of the city to a house with a dining room, I ditched it and made it into an office-sitting room. All our dinners are now in the kitchen, in among the mess and steam – I love it that way. Dining rooms are not redundant, though. One of my friends gives wonderful Saturday night dinners in hers then shuts the door on it, happily announcing that she never clears it up until Monday.

TIMING

Every person goes at their own pace so I have not given preparation times for individual recipes. Recipe books written by professionals tend to underestimate real time for everyone. Some people are a whizz at chopping and peeling, others slow and methodical. Some are very organised and get everything in a row swiftly, while others need more time to dig out that jar of spice or find the can opener.

Making a recipe for the first time always takes longer. Most of the recipes in this book are easy and very practical but some techniques need practice before they become second nature. Rolling pastry and lining tart tins, layering a terrine, kneading dough, making mayonnaise or hollandaise – such recipes can be daunting at first, but I want you to give them a go because you will get better, and faster, every time.

If at all nervous of getting things wrong in front of guests, have a practice run when cooking for yourself, or a housemate. Before you begin a recipe, scan the text for the techniques involved and have a guess at how long each will take you, then tot up the time and add a bit for contingency. When cooking, keep an eye on the time it takes to make something then build it into your planning.

Making part of or whole dishes in advance is recommended and useful for busy people who are out all day or only have limited time before a meal to cook and dress. There are many prepare-ahead recipes in this book, but also ones that are very quick to make. In the case of larger parties, I suggest doing as much cooking and setting-up as you can the day – or even days – before.

THE TABLE

They can be enviably lovely if you do have them, but matching sets of crockery, cutlery, glassware and linen impress people less than you think – or the wrong people. If you only have a few things, it does not take long to build up your arsenal.

I have amassed a collection of 'things' over time. For china, I stuck to a colour range of white and cream, because food always looks great on it – something learned through experience with food photography in the media. My shelves sag with a quirky hoard of plates, bowls and serving dishes, mainly from charity or junk shops, antiques markets and auctions (best for bargains). The joy of coming across a good find is addictive and few weeks pass without a forage.

Looking out for old linen runners and cloths is also advisable and, yes, they still look good even if they don't fit the table. Tablecloths are dispensable, but cloth napkins are something of a rule in my house. A niggle, but I strongly suggest avoiding any in a strong shade, because they can be hard to clean. My white and pale ones go in a boil wash with the bed sheets. Incidentally, you can get a sumptuous table covering effect with a white cotton flat sheet over a blanket. For glasses, my clumsiness and our stone floor dictates we only buy cheap wine glasses, though I am amazed at the quality available at little cost.

Wooden boards have also entered the vernacular of modern tableware. I like to use them often, however trendy. Large boards are expensive but pieces of kitchen worktop, cut, sanded and oiled, can look beautiful, as can more random cuts of wood. Food that can look okay in a bowl changes personality when heaped onto a board with its companion ingredients scattered around.

When it comes to table decoration, much depends on individual taste. It is your evening so use the colours and style that appeal to you. Can I suggest that, if tempted by the outlandish, you keep in mind that good food decorates itself, as I hope the images in this book will show. I like brightly candlelit tables but nothing getting in the way of other people's faces, so keep the height low. The same goes for flowers and greenery – you need to leave room for the food, so perhaps keep ornaments on the small side. At Christmas and Easter, clementines with their leaves, plump Medjool dates plus little coconut bowls (page 17) filled with shiny confectionery can stay in the centre of the table throughout the season. Choose a few of the following: gilded, sugar-coated almonds (dragees); chocolate-coated coffee beans, cubes of nougat, chocolate truffles, fruit jellies, foil-wrapped Bendick's Bittermints or gianduja (Italian hazelnut chocolates). These not only look pretty, they add a last course that you can sit nibbling, along with sips of sticky drinks, way into the small hours.

KITCHEN

The oven, surface space, fridge size, kitchen tools and gadgets will dictate what you can and cannot choose to cook. Worktop or table surface space must fit in with the planned menu. Large flat tarts will take up space, for example, while a tall casserole which can stay on the hob will not. In a small kitchen, you are more limited and need to pick space-saving recipes. I once put a pan of gravy on a chair to get it out of the way while cooking in a galley kitchen, and then heard with horror the sound of a guest's dog, slurping happily.

Consider the space inside your oven. A single oven with two shelves will be down to one when there is a large roast to cook. There will be no room for anything else. Either use the roasting joint resting time to quickly grill-roast some smaller potatoes or other vegetables, or sauté them on the hob. This becomes common sense but it is always a good idea to think about the schedule beforehand so the cooking period is not stressful and the food is ready more or less when you want it to be. If the oven space is limited, make cold appetisers and serve cheese or a cake made the day before for dessert. There are many puddings which can be made in advance – for example, crème caramel (page 142) is convenient because it can be made at least a day before.

There is purity to a handmade dinner constructed with basic tools, but regular host-cooks will long to save time when they can. My kitchen has its 'investment gadgets'. A powerful food processor is a kitchen's battle tank, not only making cutting and blending light work, but also the difference between choosing a recipe and not. Smooth and velvety soups, sauces and purées would be impossible without this machine, which has earned its keep many times over in the time it has given back.

I still have my hand-held electric whisk from 20 years ago but have since bought a KitchenAid, a mighty stand mixer, which sturdily beats, kneads and whisks. It is an impressive piece of equipment and an investment. It is possible to make meringue or buttercream with a cheap hand whisk but you will have to knead your own yeast dough, which for some is a sensual and rewarding exercise.

Indispensable hand tools include a good-quality cook's knife with a 20cm blade for chopping; a serrated knife; one for paring and another for filleting. Please buy a good carving knife, with fork and steel to sharpen it with. You cannot underestimate the satisfaction taken from the ability to slice good meat finely. Sawing away at food when in the throes of trying to get it onto the table is harrowing. You bought a beautiful piece of meat, cooked it perfectly and now it looks as if it has been attacked . . . Bad knives waste food. Add to your batterie de cuisine a sharp U-shaped peeler, a mandolin for cutting wafer-thin slices, a julienne cutter and a pair of durable kitchen scissors. For suppliers, see the directory on page 268.

For large numbers I have a 'party pan', a large-capacity saucepan with a lid in which I can make enough food for forty. These are available from catering suppliers and also from Asian markets, where they are very good value for money. If you love to throw parties, a big pan takes a lot of hassle out of the cooking. I store mine in the understairs cupboard. For storing bigger quantities of food for parties, I buy inexpensive plastic bedding containers with lids from hardware shops. These are shallow and make mixing salads or other cold food an easy task.

DISPOSABLES

The new generation of 'eco' disposable plates, bowls and serving dishes, made from biodegradable materials such as compressed palm leaves or coconut shell, have transformed my larger dinners and parties. At our children's summer party (see Summertime feast, page 196) we used them for all courses instead of hiring crockery. It was simpler and cheaper, and fitted in well with the style of this event, a sit-down dinner in a tent. Being able to dispose of everything at the end of the evening was a boon. They are a far cry from the bendy paper plates or gaudy plastic picnic-ware of the past and now come in every conceivable size and shape. Suppliers also stock bamboo skewers, cornstarch cutlery and other biodegradables, and will deliver (see page 272).

HIRE

Hiring crockery, plates and glassware for large numbers is something I always feel nervous about. Although an online search will turn up a fresh number of hire firms who specialise in vintage tableware and linen, the catalogue of most others is basic. If the party is as important as a wedding or other major event, it is worth taking the trouble to visit the hire firm – or firms – and look at samples, to be sure that you are happy with what they have available. If you are drinking special wine, for example, you might want glasses with fine rims, not ones with edges like pie dishes.

Hired tableware has not moved on much from 'station hotel' style. Crockery tends to be clunky, usually white or white with a gilt rim; cutlery is dark grey stainless steel and the tablecloths grey-white and synthetic, the whole lot making tables look impersonal. Some larger hire firms have ranges for different budgets, but prices for the best quality are considerably more. It is the same with furniture. If you want traditional-style wooden chairs, instead of plastic folding types, costs will be higher.

Check all the details and terms. Be aware of hidden charges, usually for delivery, cleaning fees and also breakages. Most of this will be on a pro forma invoice. You will have to return or sign an agreement, which will allow the hire firm to deduct losses or breakages.

Kitchenware is also available to rent, from large containers to induction hobs and trolleys. You can also hire catering-size charcoal barbecues, giant ice bins for drinks, fish kettles and coffee-making equipment.

For music, simple speaker systems – if you don't have one already – can be hired that work with smartphones and tablets. They are easy – even for technophobes like me – to set up.

WEATHER

If giving a party in a home with not enough shelter for the number invited, plan on the assumption that it will rain. For smaller parties buy a cheap gazebo. For larger, tent and marquee hire companies, who also supply gazebos and 'kitchen tents', will quote in advance when you supply details of the space and number of guests – expect to pay quite a bit to rent a marquee. If you have a specific image of what you want, make sure to ask for details such as the tent material. For example, if you want an old-fashioned canvas with wooden poles and guy ropes, be exact about this.

You will be asked to measure the space to see what will fit. Thanks to a blossoming of festivals over the last decade, it is now possible to hire a much greater variety of tents. Gorgeous embroidered tents from India with batik linings; teepees, old khaki military tents and 'stretch' tents – which are excellent for any surface or strange-shaped gardens – are hirable more or less nationwide. The same companies will also be able to supply accessories like rugs, ottomans and cushions.

HELP

There are no medals for doing everything. If offered help, always accept; I cannot bear to see a host doing it all unless they have everything under control and make it look genuinely effortless. A sweating cook, dashing about with drinks when the toast is burning yet refusing help, sets everyone on edge. Let someone make toast and another refill glasses – they love it. Early guests are good at the last-minute things we think will be done before everyone gets there: washing salad leaves, hulling strawberries, or washing up pans.

There is often someone who is better at carving roasts than anyone else and loves to show it – let them. Help with serving and clearing is welcome, but I don't necessarily like to enslave people to wash up straight after dinner because it can break up an evening. There is that happy point in an evening when people just want to sit, chat and drink – and I want to be there, too.

Enlisting a more formal kind of paid help can be as simple as offering cash to someone's teenager, rather than using an agency. They will likely leap at it and are usually very good at recruiting others, too. Always make sure that you have enough people to clear up.

HOW TO FOLLOW THE RECIPES

Before using this book, please be familiar with the following:

SALT

'Sea Salt' – soft crystal salt that can be crumbled between forefinger and thumb.

'Salt' – fine table salt, ideally sea salt, or fine ground rock salt.

OILS

Olive Oil – use extra virgin, cold pressed oil unless specified.

Vegetable Oil – preferably groundnut or grapeseed oil for dressings or mayonnaise. Alternatively use rapeseed oil or sunflower oil. In cooking you can substitute vegetable oil for duck fat or pork fat.

SMALL, MEDIUM OR LARGE

A medium onion or potato is the size of a snooker ball. Small is the size of a ping pong ball or smaller and large like an average orange.

Tablespoons, Dessertspoons & Teaspoons – level unless specified 'heaped.'

TEMPERATURE & TIMING

All oven temperatures vary. The given temperatures and timings are for my own fan oven. For roasting I use a setting that combines fan oven with grill. You will need to adapt to using your own electric oven, gas oven or Aga. If you feel uncertain, buy a good quality oven thermometer.

WEIGHTS & MEASURES

Tablespoon and teaspoon measures are level unless specified.

Note that in some recipes, liquids are weighed not measured in a jug.

A 'pinch' is as much as you can pick up with forefinger and thumb.

A handful - all you can grab. With herbs it is leaves only, not stalks.

CONVERSIONS

Weights: Metric – Imperial		Volume: Metric – Imperial	
5g	1/8 oz	1.25 ml	¼ tsp.
10g	¼oz	2.5 ml	½ tsp.
15g	½oz	5 ml	1 tsp.
25–30g	1oz	10 ml	2 tsp.
55g	2oz	15 ml	1 tbsp.
85g	3oz	30ml	2 tbsp/1 fluid oz
115	4oz	50 ml	2 fl oz
140g	5oz	60 ml	4 tbsp.
175g	6oz	100ml	3.5 fluid oz
200g	7oz	125ml	4 fluid oz
225g	8oz	200ml	7 fluid oz/⅓ pint
250g	9oz	300ml	10 fluid oz/½ pint
280g	10oz	500ml	18 fluid oz
350g	12oz	568ml	20 fluid oz/1 pint
375g	13oz	1 litre	1.75 pints
400g	14oz		
425g	15oz		
450g	1lb		
1kg	2lb 4oz		
2kg	4lb 8oz		

US Cups – Metric – Imperial

1 cup flour	150g	5oz
1 cup white sugar	225g	8oz
1 cup butter/lard	225g	8oz
1 cup ground almonds	110g	4oz
1 cup rice	200g	7oz
1 stick butter	110g	4oz

DINNER

FIRST COURSES

MEAT AND FISH

If you and your friends love good meat and fish, the first course of dinner can be a chance to eat something a little special: a layered pork and game terrine to eat with hot toast and fruity pickles; matured beef fillet, sparing yet satisfying, cut thin for carpaccio; or perhaps fresh crab from the south coast with its delicate marine flavour. Small tasters of fine or unusual ingredients create a sense of occasion and, if they are specialities sourced close to where you live, they add an element of the locality – a sense of place.

That is not to say you cannot make something beautiful to open the dinner using humble, everyday ingredients. It depends how you go about it. Chicken livers whipped up to make a light and smooth cream are pure elegance, for example, and a shining ham hock terrine the prettiest pink and green centrepiece.

The following recipes based on meat and fish are a collection gathered over years. Some are quite retro, others more the food of now, but all share the same attitude in that they are practical, reasonably modest in terms of cost, yet visually striking. Many are dishes to hand from person to person, ice-breakers that bring common warmth between people who may only just have met.

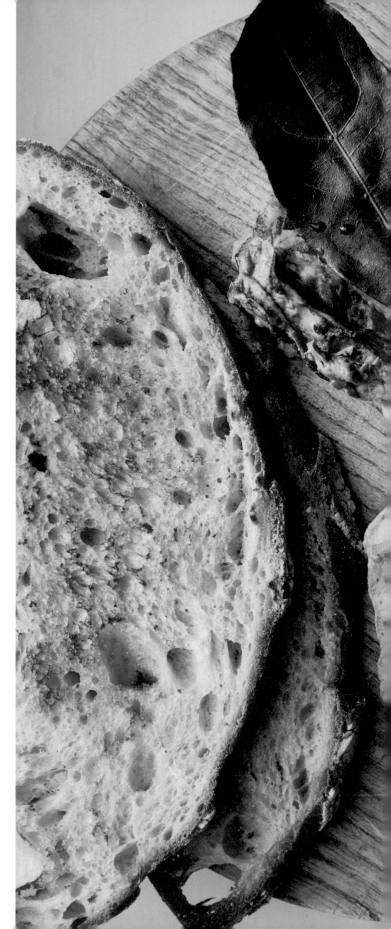

Many should be eaten at room temperature, because it is simply so much easier to start a meal with something that is ready when there may well be finishing work to do on a main course. Almost all are adaptable, in that you can vary some ingredients depending on season or their availability, but essentially this group should have among it recipes that you can rely on time and time again.

It is only fair to add that there is a group of 'ad hoc' starters that do not need precise recipes: 'deli' items like smoked salmon and other fish, or perhaps charcuterie, which need only a basket of bread, something pickled, or, in the case of air-dried ham, fresh fruit like ripe figs, pears, peach or melon. Be creative: you can make these starters up as you go along and, with the addition of a few fresh herbs or salad leaves, a splash of extra virgin olive oil or a cut lemon, they become a handsome first course.

POTTED CRAB

with Melba toast

Serves: 6–8

Serving dish: individual pots or shallow dish or bowl (500ml capacity)

150g brown crabmeat

300g white crabmeat

grated zest and juice of ½ lemon

½ tsp ground mace

¼–½ tsp cayenne pepper

salt, to taste

150g salted butter

finely chopped chives, thyme leaves or fennel fronds, to garnish

To serve:

8 slices brown bread

Tabasco sauce

If this were not such a winning, people-pleasing plate of food I think my friends would have become weary of potted crab given the number of times they've been served it. I make it with a combination of white and brown crabmeat, two parts of white to one of brown, but you can make it with only white if you prefer a less rich mix. Fresh crab is rarely sold in supermarkets non-pasteurised – which will diminish the flavour. You can usually buy fresh picked crab from independent fishmongers, or from online fish specialists (see Directory, page 269).

In a bowl mix together the crabmeat, lemon zest and juice, and spices. Taste for seasoning. Transfer the crabmeat into the pots or shallow bowl, smooth the surface but do not pat it down to compact the meat.

Melt the butter in a small saucepan. Let it bubble for 30 seconds, but make sure it doesn't burn. The butter will separate, with white whey sinking to the bottom, and there will be some foam on top. Pass it through a sieve lined with a sheet of kitchen towel and placed over a jug – this will remove the white solids. Then pour the clarified butter over the crab. Scatter over a few chives, thyme leaves or fennel fronds, to make it look pretty, then put the dish in the fridge for 30 minutes, to set. It is now ready to eat.

The Melba toast can be part-prepared up to 24 hours in advance, kept in a container and crisped up just before serving. Toast the bread as normal then cut off the crusts. Run a knife horizontally through the bread, so you have two thin slices. Cut each into two triangles.

A few minutes before serving, preheat the oven to 180°C/fan 160°C/350°F/ Gas 4. Put the thin triangles on a baking sheet and bake for approximately 8 minutes until crisp and curled. To serve, wrap the toasts in a napkin to keep them warm. Serve with the potted crab, and put some Tabasco on the table.

Options: Substitute the crab for spider crabmeat, lobster meat or cooked shrimps or prawns.

LITTLE LYONNAISE SALAD

Serves: 6–8

Serving dish: individual shallow bowls or a large platter

1kg salad potatoes

½ tsp salt

1 apple, sliced very thin

juice of 1 lemon

12 rashers thin-cut smoked back bacon

8 slices smooth black pudding, skin removed

4 tbsp roast pork, cut into bite-size pieces (optional)

3 handfuls red (or green) chicory leaves

4 sprigs tarragon, leaves

2 tbsp chopped flat-leaf parsley or chervil

2 tbsp cornichons,

1 tbsp capers, rinsed

4 eggs, boiled and peeled

For the dressing:

1 heaped tbsp Dijon mustard

1 tsp sugar

2 tsp red wine vinegar

2 tbsp water

large pinch of salt

1 garlic clove, halved

6 tbsp sunflower oil

2 tbsp extra virgin olive oil

A consoling starter with a punchy, mustardy dressing that will fill hungry people and has all the elements carnivores enjoy: bacon and black pudding, potatoes, tangy chicory, herbs and piquant pickles. A little heap of this attractive pink and green salad in chilly weather makes a great opener, but you could also double the quantities for a supper or lunch main course.

Put all the dressing ingredients in a bowl and mix together well until you have a thick emulsion. Allow the dressing to sit for 30 minutes or so, so the garlic infuses.

Put the potatoes in a large pan, cover with water and add the salt then bring to the boil. Cook until the potatoes are just tender and a bit waxy in the centre. Drain and refresh with cold water then leave to cool a little. Cut the potatoes into quarters, then set to one side in a warm place.

Toss the apple slices in lemon juice and set to one side. Slowly fry the bacon until crisp then drain on kitchen paper. Break into shards and set aside in a warm place. Fry the black pudding then break into lumps and set aside in a warm place. If you have some leftover roast pork, quickly stir-fry the pieces in a little of the bacon fat and set aside with the other meats.

To assemble the salad, put the potatoes and meats in a large bowl and briefly toss together with half the dressing. Transfer to a large serving platter or individual bowls then scatter over the apple, chicory, tarragon and parsley. Cut the cornichons in half, lengthways, roughly chop the capers, and scatter these over the other ingredients. Slice the boiled eggs and share between the plates. Season, then add the remaining dressing.

Options: Substitute the roast pork with smoked or cured pork or duck. You can also use, shredded radicchio or similar (frisée, Tardivo, Treviso, Castelfranco) instead of chicory leaves.

HAM, CIDER AND WATERCRESS TERRINE
with mustard mayonnaise and carrot pickle

Serves: 6–8

**Serving dish: 2-litre container
– bowl, terrine dish, oval
pie dish**

For simmering:

2kg boneless gammon
 (raw ham)

2 bay leaves

2 sprigs thyme

2 sprigs parsley

2 sprigs tarragon

8 peppercorns

2cm-piece cinnamon stick

2 litres cider

To assemble:

8 gelatine leaves

leaves stripped from 2
 bunches watercress

For the carrot pickle:

2 large carrots, grated

1 apple, grated

4 garlic cloves, chopped

3cm-piece fresh ginger,
 peeled and grated

200ml white wine vinegar

200g demerara sugar

125g flaked almonds

1 tsp yellow mustard seeds

1 tsp ground coriander
 seeds

For the mayonnaise:

1 tbsp Dijon mustard

3 egg yolks

A ham terrine and its accompanying pickle and mayonnaise makes a great first course for big eaters. Easy and economical, it is an ideal recipe for an occasion where you need to prepare food in advance. On the day, just turn it out onto a plate, put on the table with lots of bread or toast, then let people help themselves. Serve the pickle and mayonnaise on the side – and offer seconds and thirds. This recipe provides easily enough for eight people, but I like to make a large terrine so I have leftovers, useful to dip into for the next day or two. For ease, I suggest lining the dish or container with clingfilm but if you are confident that you can unmould the terrine by dipping the dish in warm water, it gives it a lovely, clear and shiny appearance.

Put the gammon in a large pan and cover with water. Bring to the boil and drain – this helps draw the salt out of the cured meat. Put the gammon back in the pan and add all the simmering ingredients – herbs, spices and cider.

Bring back to simmering point and cook for 2–2½ hours, until the meat is tender enough to mash with a fork. Remove from the heat and drain – reserving the stock, which must then be passed through a fine sieve. Set the stock to one side.

Put the gelatine in a bowl and cover with cold water. Leave for a few minutes then squeeze out the water. Put 200ml of the stock in a pan and add the softened gelatine. Warm gently, swirling the pan to dissolve the gelatine – do *not* let it boil or the gelatine will not set. Add 600ml more of the stock and whisk for a second or two.

Line a shallow dish with a large sheet of clingfilm. Pull or the ham into pieces. Put it in the dish and add the watercress leaves. Mix lightly and add enough of the stock and gelatine mixture to just cover the contents of the dish, no more. Place in the fridge for several hours to set. Once set, cover with clingfilm.

150ml groundnut or sunflower oil

30ml extra virgin olive oil

1 tbsp finely chopped capers

1 tsp lemon juice

pinch of ground white pepper

pinch of fine sea salt

To serve:

extra sprigs of fresh watercress

a few small capers

toast or bread and butter

To make the carrot pickle, put all the ingredients in a pan, bring to the boil then cook for about 15 minutes, stirring occasionally, until thick and sticky like chutney.

To make the mayonnaise, put the mustard and eggs in a bowl and whisk together by hand or electric mixer. Gradually whisk in the groundnut oil until all is incorporated and the sauce is thick and gloopy. Finally beat in the olive oil, capers, lemon juice, white pepper and salt.

Unmould the terrine, turning it out onto a flat serving plate then peeling off the clingfilm. Throw the spare watercress over the surface, scatter over the extra capers and serve with toast or bread and butter.

Option: Flat-leaf parsley (leaves only) can be used in place of the watercress.

THREE CARPACCIOS

*The following three recipes are easy-going, picturesque starter dishes that can
be adapted to suit the seasons. Given a sharp knife or a mandolin, which can slice
almost any food thin as gossamer, 'carpaccio' is possibly one of the easiest things
to make, and possibly the most gorgeous to look at. It's a borrowed term, of course.
What was once a recipe for filmy raw beef served with Parmesan and a mustardy
mayonnaise now stretches to all things cut thin. It has great advantages for dinner
planning. You can prepare about two hours before you eat, covering flat plates until
they look like an edible mosaic, then protect them with clingfilm and put in the fridge
until needed – bits of pretty embellishment can be added just before you serve.*

*Carpaccio dishes are very adaptable. If you have not got all the ingredients in these
recipes, you can play with them within reason. For example, I added some fresh
wasabi to one dish but you could easily use finely sliced radish. These recipes are also
relatively economical, given that they are small quantities of rich foods. The only
serious rule is to use raw materials that are at their peak of freshness or best quality
– good extra virgin olive oil is a must, by the way.*

*One last notable point – carpaccio is easy but you will need to practise slicing food
thin and buy a suitable knife. Meat and fish are easier to slice with a knife that has
a long blade, like single-bevelled Yanagi knives used for cutting sashimi (see
Directory, page 272). These vary in price but an online search will turn up knives
that are good value for money and which, if properly cared for, will cut your
sashimi for years to come.*

1. WHITE FISH AND AVOCADO

Serves: 6–8

Serving dish: 6–8 large dinner plates, as flat as possible

500g skinless fillet of sea bream, hake, halibut or other white fish

2–3 ripe, firm avocados

4 handfuls of peppery small-leaf salad preferably with red-green chard, sorrel, watercress or mizuna

12 violet flower heads or other edible flowers (optional, when in season)

2 tsp shaved fresh wasabi (see Directory, page 270) or 12 radishes, sliced very thin – lengthways if French radishes

To serve:

toasted sesame oil and extra virgin olive oil

2 tsp poppy seeds

soft-crystal sea salt flakes, smoked or natural

The fish in this version of carpaccio is raw, as for sashimi, so be careful to buy fish that is guaranteed fresh. Either go to a trusted fishmonger, buy frozen online or check the fish on supermarket wet fish counters for glossy, wet skin and bright eyes. Ask the fishmonger to fillet the fish for you.

Certain white fish have the right sweetness and clear flavours for carpaccio: sea bream is easily available, but you can also use hake, halibut, brill or (if you are feeling extravagant) turbot. Yellow tail is an exotic fish with a dense texture that the Japanese worship as a sashimi fish and is available frozen online, but in the photograph is arctic char, a salmon relative with a pink-white flesh and the flavour of sea trout. This is farmed in the UK, coincidentally in the village where I live. For details of how to buy arctic char and also frozen fish online, suitable for eating raw, see the directory on page 269.

Put the fish fillet in the freezer for 30–40 minutes to firm it up and put the plates in a cool place, preferably the fridge or in a basin with water and ice to make sure they are nice and cool.

When firm, use a very sharp knife with a long blade to cut thin strips of the fish – about 2mm maximum thickness. Divide the fish among the plates, evenly spaced all over the surface. Having done this you can cover the plates with clingfilm and store them in the fridge for up to 2 hours to save preparation at the last minute.

Before serving (no more than 30 minutes prior), cut the avocado into thin – approximately 2mm – slices and, similarly, distribute it around the plates. Scatter over the leaves, flowers (if using) and wasabi or radishes. Finally, drip small droplets of sesame oil over the plates (no more than a teaspoon overall), then the olive oil – about 2 teaspoons max per plate. Follow with a scattering of a few poppy seeds and sea salt flakes.

Options: Finely smoked halibut in place of raw fish, or cooked white crab meat.

2. BEEF
with red leaves and ewe's milk cheese
Serves: 6

Serving dish: 6 large dinner plates, as flat as possible, or individual boards

750g dry-aged rump steak in one piece, or beef fillet

olive oil, for rubbing

dried thyme leaves

freshly ground black pepper

200g red salad leaves (radicchio, red chicory or special leaves like bull's blood, red sorrel, baby red chard, pink stem radish cress or red radish cress – see Directory, page 268)

200g hard ewe's milk cheese (pecorino, Lord of the Hundreds, Berkswell or manchego)

1 tbsp chopped chives or chive flower petals (when in season)

6 tbsp extra virgin olive oil

sea salt flakes, smoked or natural

You do not have to use expensive beef fillet, although it is the most tender and easy to prepare. Beef carpaccio's inventor at Harry's Bar in Venice recommends 'shell' steak, which is the American equivalent of lower rump steak. Ask the butcher to cut a 500g piece from well-hung (dry-aged) rump and trim it of fat and any membrane or gristle. Don't try cutting slices from individually cut steaks or you will just waste a lot.

Trim the beef of any membrane or fat. Rub some olive oil on the surface, sprinkle with dried thyme leaves and season with plenty of black pepper. Heat a pan until very hot then sear the beef on both sides very quickly, rolling it around in the pan until browned – this should take just a few seconds.

Remove from the pan, put on a plate and transfer to the freezer until the beef nearly reaches freezing point, 45–60 minutes. Then, with your sharp knife, slice or shave some thin slices, no more than 2mm thick.

If your slices are not wafer-thin enough to pull apart with a fork, place them between two sheets of baking parchment and use a meat hammer or a rolling pin to flatten them further. Make sure to hammer evenly for best results. Carefully lift off the paper before dividing the slices among the plates.

Shred the red leaves if they are large. Pare the cheese using a mandolin or potato peeler. Distribute it on top of the beef on each plate, followed by the leaves and chives or chive flowers. Finally, zigzag the extra virgin olive oil over the plates *just before* you serve your guests. Scatter over sea salt and black pepper.

Options: Substitute the beef for venison loin or veal loin (good with an anchovy-based dressing).

3. FENNEL AND APPLE
with toasted walnut pesto

Serves: 6–8

Serving dish: 6–8 large dinner plates, as flat as possible

250g walnut halves

olive oil, for toasting

100g Parmesan, Grana Padano or Berkswell cheese, finely grated

4 tbsp finely chopped flat-leaf parsley

8 tbsp extra virgin olive oil

salt and freshly ground black pepper

2–3 fennel bulbs, as fresh as possible

juice of 1 lemon

4 dessert apples (Cox's, Worcester, Russets, Braeburn or Granny Smith)

To serve:

extra virgin olive oil

sea salt flakes, smoked or natural

Raw fennel has a strong taste of aniseed which mellows, becoming fruity, when the slices are marinated in lemon juice, and it is exceptionally attractive when sliced. Ideally you need a mandolin for slicing the fennel, but a very sharp knife and your skills will also do. Cut it too thick and it is difficult to eat raw, however, so it must be transparently thin. Choose extra-fresh, firm fennel bulbs with a shiny skin and healthy green fronds. This salad is also one I serve as a side dish to baked, fried or grilled fish.

Put the walnuts in a pan with 1 dessertspoon of olive oil and very gently toast until fragrant and golden – be careful, because walnuts burn easily. Remove from the heat and tip onto a plate to cool completely. When cool, mix in a bowl with the cheese, parsley and extra virgin olive oil, season to taste with salt and freshly ground black pepper, and set to one side.

Remove any hard, dry-ish or discoloured outer layers of the fennel bulbs and reserve the fronds. If the base of the bulbs is at all brown, use a potato peeler to trim it. Slice the fennel on a mandolin or very finely with a knife. Place in a bowl and toss in the lemon juice and a pinch of salt. Leave for 10 minutes for the flavours to combine.

Meanwhile, cut the flesh off the apple, leaving behind the core and keeping the skin on. Slice the apples very thinly on a mandolin or with a knife. Divide the apple slices between the plates, followed by the fennel, then drop little teaspoonfuls of the walnut pesto onto each plate. Finally, scatter over the reserved fennel fronds, a few more drops of extra virgin olive oil and some sea salt flakes. Then serve.

Options: Kohlrabi or dukon radish in place of fennel; pears in place of apples; dill or chervil leaves in place of fennel fronds, to serve.

FISH CAKES
with lemongrass and coriander

Serves: 6–8

800g boneless, skinless white
    fish fillet (haddock, cod,
    plaice, monkfish or other)

2 egg whites

4 garlic cloves, grated

2 tbsp chopped coriander
    leaves

2 tbsp very finely sliced
    lemongrass

1 tbsp fish sauce

salt and freshly ground black
    pepper

groundnut or sunflower oil,
    for shallow frying

For the salad and dressing:

4 handfuls of mixed salad
    leaves

4 sprigs coriander, leaves
    only

a few radishes, sliced

2 tbsp Shaoxing wine

1 tbsp fish sauce

4 tbsp fresh lime juice

2 tbsp light soy sauce

1 tbsp honey

Tangy, herby fishcakes with an enjoyably bouncy texture – an easy recipe with plenty of contemporary appeal. It is great for novice hosts, but because the cakes are fried at the last minute, this starter should ideally be followed by something that is ready, like slow-roasted pork shoulder, resting in the oven – which it will go very well with. Alternatively, put on the table as part of a sharing menu.

Roughly chop the fish by hand or in a food processor, until it is a lumpy mash, then put it in a bowl and mix with the egg whites, garlic, coriander, lemongrass and fish sauce. Season with a pinch of salt and pepper.

Shape 14–16 cakes with two dessertspoons: scoop up one spoonful of the mixture then transfer it to the other spoon. Repeat this a couple of times and you will have a smooth, oval lozenge or 'quenelle' shape. Place on a plate then repeat with the remaining mixture until it is all used up.

Combine the salad leaves, coriander and radishes. Put the Shaoxing wine, fish sauce, lime juice, soy sauce and honey into a small bowl or cup and whisk together. Set to one side.

Heat the oil in a large frying pan until it sizzles when you add a small pinch of the fishcake mixture. Fry the fishcakes on all sides for about 3 minutes, until golden brown – keep the hob heat moderate; do not let the oil get too hot. Drain on kitchen paper then serve with the salad in individual bowls. Spoon some dressing over each and serve straight away.

Option: Replace the white fish with roughly chopped raw prawn meat.

ROAST BONE MARROWS
with parsley-caper relish and toast

Serves: 6

Serving dish: boards or individual plates

6 marrow bones, about 20cm long, split lengthways (more if your guests are the hungry carnivore type)

sea salt and freshly ground black pepper

For the parsley-caper relish:

150g flat-leaf parsley, leaves only

2 tbsp capers, small or large, chopped

pinch of white pepper

1 tsp honey

juice of ½ lemon

To serve:

6 or more slices of white sourdough bread

The starter meat lovers will love and remember you for. Bone marrow is the most unctuous, full-flavoured component of beef and needs very little embellishment after roasting except toast to soak it up and parsley to cut its incredible richness. It is very easy to prepare, and even comes in its own natural container! The new-found popularity of bone marrow has seen it come ready-prepared in some supermarkets, but if you prearrange with your butcher's, they will reserve and split the marrow bones for you.

Preheat the oven to 190°C/fan 170°C/375°F/Gas 5. The split marrow bones will reveal the pale pink matter inside the bone. Season with salt and pepper, then place in a roasting pan cut side up. Roast for about 20–30 minutes until the bones are golden and the marrow soft. Do not over-roast or the marrow will render away, leaving the bones empty and the pan full of fat.

Once roasted, you can keep the bones warm in the switched-off oven while you prepare the relish and toast. Mix together the relish ingredients just before you eat, leaving the lemon juice until last to stop the parsley discolouring.

Toast the bread – no butter is needed – then serve immediately.

PORK, DUCK AND PISTACHIO TERRINE

Serves: 6–8

Serving dish: 1-litre terrine dish or loaf tin

30g butter
1 garlic clove, finely chopped
1 large shallot, chopped
300g pork shoulder meat, cut into 1cm chunks
500g pork mince
1 tsp thyme leaves
1 tsp salt
½ tsp fresh ground black pepper
60ml port
1 egg, beaten
30g softened butter, for greasing
16 slices pancetta
6 soft dried figs, halved
70g unsalted pistachio nuts
1 x 200g duck breast, or two smaller ones, cut into long strips along the grain of the meat
2 bay leaves

To serve:

bowl of pickle or chutney (good-quality bought – see Directory, page 268 – or homemade: try the easy Carrot Pickle on page 32, or Olive and Fig Pickle on page 178)
cornichons (pickled baby gherkins)
hot toast and butter

Adaptable through the seasons and easy enough for large numbers, I love to make baked terrines like this one. They look so 'brown' in the pot after baking but when you cut that first slice, to reveal a mosaic of shell-pink and buff-coloured meats threaded with nuts and/or preserved fruits, it feels like just reward for the initial patience needed to 'build' the terrine. It is very important to buy free-range pork mince and meat for a terrine, because intensively reared pork releases a white liquid during cooking, overly shrinking the terrine.

Think of the following recipe as a 'blueprint', which can be modified through the seasons – see the options opposite.

Preheat the oven to 200°C/fan 180°C/400°F/Gas 6. Melt the butter in a pan and add the garlic and shallot. Cook for 2 minutes over a medium heat until soft, cool for a few minutes then put in a bowl with the pork, the thyme, salt, pepper and port. Leave to marinate for 1 hour then mix in the egg.

Rub the inside of the terrine dish with the softened butter then line it neatly with 12 of the pancetta slices, laying them side by side across the width of the dish and allowing them to hang down the outer side, ready to wrap around the contents later. Pack one half of the marinated pork mixture into the terrine.

Push half of the fig halves into the pork mix in the terrine – so that they run in a line the length of the dish – then do the same with half of the pistachios. Next, lay the duck breast strips lengthways along the dish. Cover with a 1cm-layer of the pork mix then another line of fig halves and the remaining pistachios. Finally, cover with the remaining pork mix, heaping it higher in the centre of the terrine to make a loaf shape.

Place the bay leaves on top, then bring the pancetta (hanging down the side of the dish) up and over the contents, wrapping them. The terrine is now ready to bake.

Cover the dish with a lid or foil and place it in a roasting tin containing 3cm of boiling hot water. Bake for 1¼–1½ hours until the meat has shrunk a little from the side of the dish. Add more water to the pan if it evaporates during cooking.

Remove the terrine from the oven and leave to cool. You will notice how the juices around the meat are reabsorbed as it cools. Chill until needed, wrapped in foil.

To serve, use a spatula to lift the terrine out of the dish. With a very sharp carving knife, cut a 2cm-thick slice for each person. Serve with hot buttered toast and pickles.

Options: For duck, use lean skinless fillets of any game bird, venison loin, chicken, rabbit, pork loin or the cheaper tenderloin or wild boar. For pistachios, use walnuts or hazelnuts; for dried figs, use dried plums; for port, use wine, cider, gin or sherry. Apple juice can also be used in place of alcohol.

VEGETABLE
AND DAIRY

Sometimes our menu choices are made for us by the seasons, and it is only common sense to open a meal celebrating the arrival of a glut. Asparagus, wild garlic, fresh peas and beans, courgette flowers, tomatoes, squash, wild mushrooms, red chicory or endives – any of these can be a pretty salad to serve with shavings of cheese, a few young leaves, toasted nuts and a zigzag of good oil or melted butter. You can play with vegetables as if arranging a mosaic, and never go wrong.

I understand that it can be difficult to find vegetables that are really fresh and perky from being just picked. In the abundant growing season, May to November, look up the location and date of the nearest farmers' market and pay a visit. The vegetables from the market are so fresh that even if you are not expecting people for a week, they will keep well if carefully wrapped in damp newspaper and put in a bag in the fridge.

Not all vegetable starters have to be made from fresh produce, however. I love to make butter bean purée and crispy flatbreads not just because they go down so well but they are a good economical choice – you can literally make masses of this for the masses, and providing it is well presented it will be appreciated by the masses, too.

Both vegetable and dairy starters solve another problem – making sure everyone is happy. With larger gatherings you can almost guarantee someone will not appreciate a meat or fish starter, so instead of making alternatives you can please all with one recipe.

By 'dairy' I mean cheese, and the wide availability of sublime fresh cheese like buffalo mozzarella, burrata and other fresh, sweet cheeses made from goat or ewe's milk, give plenty of quick and easy starter options when you are short of time. It is really worth seeking out the best, artisan versions of these foods, as a little will go a long way.

The following are favourite recipes, appearing time and time again at my suppers. Sometimes it is nice to mix them, offering two to three recipes when you have a larger number of guests. All are vegetarian but combine well with meat or fish dishes, too.

ASPARAGUS WITH HOLLANDAISE

Serves: 6–8

Serving dish: individual plates, with jug or sauceboat for the hollandaise

½ tsp salt
800g asparagus

For the hollandaise:

1 tsp white peppercorns
1 tsp white wine vinegar
3 tbsp (45ml) water
4 egg yolks
200g unsalted butter
juice of ½ lemon
pinch of fine sea salt

Take courage because, contrary to rumours, divinely smooth and rich hollandaise sauce is not difficult to make and you will not be sweating over it at the last moment. This recipe is one often used by restaurants because it can be made in advance and stored in a wide-necked Thermos or in a container placed over a bath of warm water. I have suggested a generous amount of asparagus in this recipe because I love it, but if serving a very rich second course, it is fine to reduce it to 120g prepared asparagus for each person.

To make the hollandaise, put the peppercorns, vinegar and water in a pan, bring to boiling point, then strain into a mixing bowl. Add the egg yolks and beat until thick and foamy – preferably using an electric whisk. Then, a little bit at a time, add the melted butter, whisking continuously. Finally, add the lemon juice and sea salt. The sauce will be the same thickness as double cream. To thicken it and warm it a little, place the bowl over a pan of barely simmering water and gently stir. Once the sauce is thick and a little warmer than blood temperature, take the bowl off the heat.

You can either store the hollandaise in a Thermos – use one with a wide neck – for up to 1½ hours, or in the pan while maintaining the water temperature at about 50°C/120°F. Keep an eye on it, and put a disc of baking parchment on the surface to prevent a skin forming.

To prepare the asparagus, pare the skin from the lower part of the stalk, because it can be quite tough unless the asparagus is very fresh. Fill a wide pan like a frying pan with 4cm of water. Bring it to the boil and add the salt. Add the asparagus spears and simmer for 5 minutes or until they are just tender – use the point of a vegetable knife to test.

RICE-PAPER GARDEN ROLLS
with cucumber, watercress and avocado, with honey and lime sauce

Serves: 6–8

Serving dish: large flat board or platter; you will need clean tea towels, for preparing the rice pancake wrappers

16 × 20cm diameter rice pancake wrappers

1½ cucumbers, deseeded and cut into 20cm × 5mm strips

the leafy tops (about 10cm) of 3 bunches of watercress

1 small bunch coriander

16 chives

3 ripe avocados, stones removed and flesh sliced lengthways

For the sauce:

2 tbsp runny honey

2 tbsp light soy sauce

2 tbsp pale dry sherry or Shaoxing wine

1 tsp red wine vinegar

8 chives, finely sliced

1 tsp toasted sesame oil

Refreshing, light and incredibly pretty starters to hand round with a dipping sauce – at the table or standing if you prefer to have the first course before sitting down. Based on Vietnamese summer rolls, they are made with rice-paper 'pancakes', which are available in supermarkets, online or from Southeast Asian or Chinese shops.

To prepare the rice sheets, soak two clean tea towels in cold water then partially wring them out. Lay one on the counter and place 4 rice pancakes onto it, side by side and not overlapping. Cover with the second towel and pat with your hand. The sheets will soften in about 10 minutes. You may need to drip a little more water onto the surface of the towels to keep them moist.

To make the sauce, mix together all the ingredients and set to one side in a small serving bowl.

To assemble the rolls, pick up a soft rice sheet – they will be flexible and soft but are quite easy to handle. Put a small handful of cucumber in a line in the centre of the rice sheet then add some avocado, also in a line. Take 2 small bunches of the watercress tops and place each with their leaves facing outwards, to the edge of the roll. Do the same with the chives.

Pick up one end of the wrapper and bring it over the heap of contents. Tuck it in and roll to make a fat 'cigar', with leaves poking out at either end. Pick up the cigar, place on another rice sheet and roll again to give it a second skin. Place on a board, under a damp towel. Repeat with all the others (you will have to soften a second batch of rice sheets).

Cut the rolls into three pieces – they will stand up on their flat end – then place on the serving platter or board with the dipping sauce alongside. Hand around or plate the rolls individually.

Options: For a fish starter add fresh white crabmeat or cooked prawns; replace the watercress with baby spinach or wild rocket.

BAKED WHOLE CHEESE
with toast spoons and chicory

Serves: 6–8

Serving dish: Large board or platter

2 whole 250g Camembert, Roblochon, Epoisses, Tunworth

4 slices sourdough bread

1 red chicory head (optional)

This is no trouble to put together and makes a great sharing starter – it is such fun to scoop gooey, stringy cheese with toast and chicory spoons. It's also a good last minute recipe in that most late night shops sell cardboard packed soft cheeses of varying types, and it matters not a jot if they aren't ripe, because they are hugely improved by baking. Note that you cannot do this with a half cheese.

Preheat the oven to 180°c/fan 160°C/350°F/Gas 4.

Unwrap the cheese and put both back in their wooden boxes. Place these on a baking sheet. Bake for 10–15 minutes until you see a slight uplift in the top rind and small cracks appear. The length of time in the oven will depend on the ripeness of the cheese you have bought: it will need a little more time in the oven if it is unripe.

Meanwhile separate the chicory leaves (if using). Toast the sourdough slices and cut them into thin strips. Plate up with the cicory leaves, then take straight to the table with the hot cheese – do not keep it waiting.

TOMATO AND MUSTARD TART

Serves: 6–8

Serving dish: large board or individual plates

plain flour, for dusting

500g all-butter puff pastry or homemade rough puff pastry (see page 166)

4 tbsp Dijon mustard

1kg mixed coloured or 'heritage' tomatoes, cut in slices and/or halved or quartered

4 tbsp extra virgin olive oil

sea salt and freshly ground black pepper

3 sprigs basil, leaves only

We always need a recipe that is a standby, one to throw together with easily accessible ingredients, and this is mine. It is economical, everyone loves it and you can make it in reasonably large quantities. I suggest that if you cannot find a variety of tomatoes, as with this one, you use sliced cherry tomatoes, which are always a little bit riper than others. Farmers' markets often sell interesting 'heritage' tomatoes and they feature more and more in supermarkets. You can also make a large tart to cut into canapé-sized portions.

Preheat the oven to 200°C/fan 180°C/400°F/Gas 6 and line a large (30 x 25cm) baking sheet, or two smaller ones, with baking parchment.

Dust the worktop with plain flour and roll out the pastry in a rectangle to fit the baking sheet – about 3mm thickness. Trim the edges with a knife. Pick the pastry up by rolling it onto the pin and unroll it onto the lined baking sheet.

With the exception of a small border around the edges, prick the tart all over with a fork to prevent the pastry rising and dislodging the tomatoes. Spread mustard all over the pastry base, again avoiding the border. Arrange the tomatoes on top, making sure they overlap each other. Brush the surface with some of the olive oil and season with salt and pepper.

Bake for about 30 minutes or until the pastry is crisp and dark gold. It should be crispy underneath because the mustard absorbs juice from the tomatoes. When it is ready, remove it from the oven and allow to cool a little.

To serve, zigzag more olive oil over the surface and scatter with the basil leaves. Cut with a sharp knife into 6 pieces.

Options: Replace the tomatoes with curls of courgette shavings or asparagus spears, then dress either after baking with parings of pecorino cheese.

BUFFALO MOZZARELLA ROLLS

with prosciutto and peach

Serves: 4–6 (32 rolls)

Serving dish: wooden board or flat plate

16 wafer-thin slices of procuitto (Parma, Serrano or other air-dried ham)

Freshly ground black pepper

2 handfuls rocket leaves

375g buffalo mozzarella cheese (3 average sized cheeses), cut into 32 pieces

2 ripe peaches (or nectarines) each cut into 16 slices

Thick, syrupy balsamic vinegar – about 1-2 tbsp.

Extra virgin olive oil – for dressing

When I feel lazy yet want to serve something with drinks that can be picked up with fingers, these rolls of prosciutto – stuffed with delicate flavoured, fresh buffalo mozzarella and honeyed, ripe peach – (photo on page 46) are a neat fit. You can make quite a few in a few minutes and they keep for up to one hour. For a more sizeable starter dish, serve a few rolls on top of warm, grilled sourdough bread. Rub the bread with a cut garlic clove then brush with extra virgin olive oil before grilling or toasting.

Lay all the slices of prosciutto on the worktop side by side. Then with a knife or scissors, cut them in half across the middle so that you have 32 pieces about 10cm x 5cm approximately. Season with pepper then lay a few rocket leaves horizontally on to one end of each piece of ham.

Place the buffalo mozzarella pieces beside the rocket leaves on the ham, with a slice of peach. With a teaspoon, drop a little drizzle of balsamic vinegar on top – not too much or it will make the rolls leaky. Roll up the ham, packing the rocket, mozzarella and peach in tightly.

Place them all on a board or flat plate, add a little more black pepper then carefully – again so not to make them messy – drip over a few drops of olive oil. If not serving immediately, cover with clingfilm and place in the fridge.

COURGETTE TART

Serves 6-8

Serving dish: wooden board

500g rough puff pastry (see
   page 166) or ready-made
   puff pastry

4–6 courgettes

3–4 tbsp extra virgin olive
   oil, plus more for dressing

20 basil leaves

salt and fresh ground black
   pepper

2 tbsp grated pecorino
   cheese or salted ricotta

A tart to serve from early summer right through to the last days before November frosts. With a buttery, flaky puff pastry base and juicy ribbons of courgettes, this is a starter with a sublime combination of taste and texture. You can also adapt to other ingredients. If you do not want to make your own pastry buy good-quality butter puff pastry.

Pre-heat the oven to 200°C/fan 180°C/400°F/Gas 6.

Cut the pastry in half. Roll each half into a long rectangle, approximately 30 x 15cm. Place on a baking sheet then prick all over with a fork except for a 1cm border along the long edge of the tarts.

Shave the courgettes into oblong slices with a potato peeler or a mandolin. Scatter all over the pastry bases except for the borders. Brush with the olive oil then bake for about 20–30 minutes until the edges and underside of the pastry are golden and the courgettes soft and slightly singed in places. Remove from the oven and allow to cool a little.

Scatter over the basil leaves, season with salt and pepper, throw over the pecorino cheese and then drip a little more olive oil over the surface. Serve at room temperature, sliced across the width of the tart.

Options: You could substitute the courgette for thinly sliced aubergine, whole asparagus, shavings of butternut squash or new potato with thyme and rosemary.

POACHED EGG AND HERB TARTLETS
with caper and lemon dressing
Serves: 6–8

Serving dish: individual
plates Equipment: 6–8 10cm
diameter tart cases, baking
beans

For the tart shells:

350g plain flour, plus extra
    for dusting

1 tsp salt

225g diced butter, from
    the fridge

110ml ice-cold water, or
    more

For the filling:

1½ tbsp small capers,
    drained on paper

4–5 tbsp extra virgin olive
    oil

1 tbsp lemon juice

6–8 eggs, as fresh as possible

6–8 handfuls of fresh herbs
    or young salad leaves:
    chervil, flat-leaf parsley,
    tarragon, dill, bronze
    fennel leaf, baby Swiss
    chard, baby spinach,
    mizuna or mibuna, rocket,
    mesclun (mixed salad
    leaves)

Quite a sophisticated starter with contrasting textures and the springtime flavours of fresh herbs. I like to serve these on special occasions when it matters to show effort. The tart cases are a bit of a challenge the first time, but I urge you to practise them because once you can do it, they are a very useful cooking skill.

To help you, the pastry recipe below is a fail-safe method for making card-thin pastry tarts with no shrinkage or thick, heavy bottoms. You can make the pastry cases the day before and warm them through before serving, so for your first attempt I advise taking some extra time so you can concentrate. After this, you will literally be able to churn out the tart cases, time and again!

Preheat the oven to 200°C/fan 180°C/400°F/Gas 6.

To make the pastry, put the flour in a large bowl with the salt and then add the butter, breaking it into pieces with your fingers. Rub the butter into the flour with your fingertips (you can also do this in a food processor) until the mixture has a breadcrumb consistency. Add the water and mix until it comes together.

Test the dough by pinching a piece between your thumb and index finger – if it feels smooth and pliable, it is perfect. If the dough breaks or splits, add a tablespoon more water. Be careful not to overmix the pastry so it becomes warm and greasy.

Wrap the pastry in clingfilm and refrigerate for at least 45 minutes. To make the pastry shells, dust the worktop with flour then cut a piece from the lump of dough and roll it into a disc 15cm in diameter and as little as 2.5mm thick. Place the pastry disc in a tart tin and press it into the base and sides. Allow the surplus to drape over the sides, prick the base with a fork a few times and place on a baking tray.

Repeat with the other 5/7 cases, then cut rounds of baking parchment and place one inside each tart case. Fill to the top of the tin with baking beans and bake for 15 minutes, or until the edges of the pastry are light brown and the bases of the tart cases are beginning to turn crisp.

Remove the baking beans and paper, then return the tart shells to the oven for 5 more minutes. When they are fully cooked, light brown and crisp all the way through, remove from the oven and allow to cool.

Gently, with your fingers, snap the surplus pastry from the edges of the tins. You can also do this with a sharp, serrated knife, but I find it is easier to snap little pieces off.

If you make the pastry cases the day before, refresh them in a warm oven – about 100°C/fan 80°C/200°F/Gas 1 – and they will taste fresh-baked.

To finish the tarts, first fry the capers in 1 tablespoon of the olive oil, then drain on kitchen paper. Put the remaining olive oil and lemon juice in a bowl and mix well. Set aside.

Next, poach the eggs in simmering unsalted water until the whites are firm but the yolks still runny*. Remove from the pan and drain the eggs on a cloth or kitchen paper – wet eggs will make the pastry soggy.

To serve, place one egg in each tartlet. Just before serving, dress the herb salad with the caper sauce, then place a heap of the salad on each tart. Eat within about 30 minutes.

*If you find poaching eggs difficult, you can always line a ramekin with clingfilm and brush the interior with groundnut oil. Crack the egg into it and then bring up the edges of the clingfilm and twist to make a little bundle with the egg inside. You can then lower the wrapped egg into simmering water and poach as usual. When the egg is done, lower the parcel into cold water then gently unwrap it.

Options: Retain the basic filling of poached egg and herbs, adding (for a meat or fish starter) fresh white crabmeat, smoked salmon or thinly sliced prosciutto di Parma or jamón Ibérico. You could also add hollandaise sauce.

SOUP

Soup is an easy and adaptable starter.
Rarely any trouble to make, swift to
serve and always a radiant reflection of
the seasons, a ladleful is a happy dish.
Some people think of soup as a mono-
coloured lake. I think it suffers from a
poor image, perhaps because of those
silent dinner parties in period dramas,
with conversation replaced by polite
sipping. But the following recipes are
about today's soups – mainly. These can
be an adventure in ravishing flavour,
divergent texture and striking colour.
Imagine an island or two in the 'lake',
with perhaps the odd pontoon or
floating object, by which I mean when
you ladle soup for dinner, serve it with
added 'value'.

This might be a velvet-textured
vegetable soup, redolent of just one
ingredient, poured either over or around
added ingredients. For example, a
peppery, green and smooth watercress
soup, poured into a bowl with a little
heap of crisp black pudding, discs of
waxy Jersey potatoes and shards of
smoked bacon. Or, why not a coral-pink-
orange tomato soup with a pile of tiny
toasted cheese sandwiches, with basil
oil drops floating around? Alternatively,
a beetroot and marrow bone broth,
served over a few slices of waxy potato
with a spoonful of chives . . . This is when
soups become surprising and exciting,
needing a fork as well as a spoon to
enjoy its varying textures.

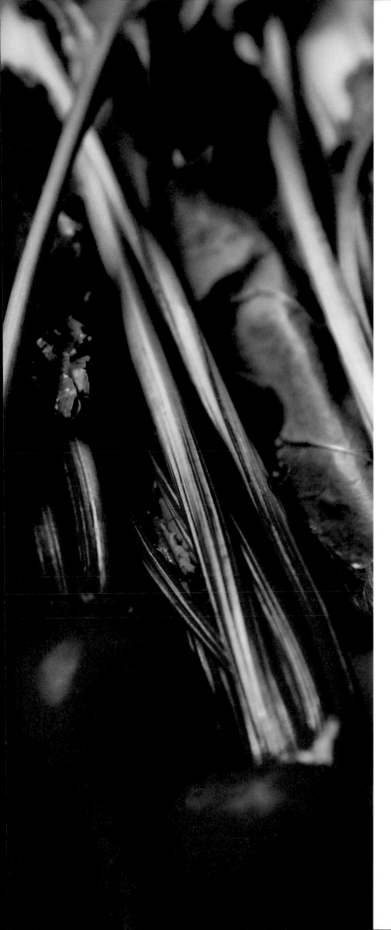

These soups are easy to make and put together, and yet they create maximum impact. There are few rules to making them, but I feel strongly that soup made with green vegetables should look fresh and green and not be left to sit around too long, losing its bright colour. To be sure of this, you can do most of the preparation in advance, leaving out the main green ingredient. In the last 30 minutes before dinner, blend either the watercress, lettuce, spinach or whatever green you are using, even if – as many have heard me do – you have to yell an apology over the electric blender din as you do so. It is all part of the fun and your guests will be merciful.

CHICKEN STOCK

Makes approximately 3 litres

1 tbsp vegetable oil

2kg chicken bones, carcass or legs/thighs/drumsticks

1 tbsp skimmed milk powder

3.5 litres water

salt

When a soup recipe asks for stock, homemade gives the best results. Stock cubes or powder are often over-salted, and sometimes contain unpleasant artificial flavourings, though you can use organic vegetable stock powder, if you have nothing else to hand. This recipe makes a good-flavoured, pale gold chicken stock, very much helped by adding a few pinches of milk powder before roasting the bones.

Preheat the oven to 180°C/fan 160°C/350°F/Gas 4. Put the oil in a casserole pan and then roll the bones around in it. Sprinkle the milk powder all over the bones. Bake until golden then remove from the oven. Cover the roasted bones with the water and simmer over a very low heat for 1½ hours. Strain and discard the bones – although we pick the meat and other bits off them for the dog – then season the stock with salt. Keeps in the fridge for about 5 days, or store in the freezer in rinsed-out plastic milk bottles. To defrost, place the bottle in a saucepan of boiling water – within 30 minutes you can use the stock.

VEGETABLE STOCK

Makes approximately 3 litres

2 kg vegetables, or raw peelings (see recipe intro), plus herbs

1 clove garlic

60g butter

3.5 litres water

salt and white pepper

You can make stock with all non-starchy vegetables that would normally be cooked. Do not add potatoes, spinach, green cabbage, or strong-flavoured vegetables that overpower, like sweet peppers or beetroot. A good base selection is onion, leek, carrot, celery, tomato, parsley, thyme, a bay leaf, leek and – for the best flavour – mushrooms or their stalks and peelings. Do experiment with others, such as fennel, Jerusalem artichokes, celeriac and cucumber. You can also add fresh apple – peelings, cores or whole – to stock.

Chop the vegetables if necessary, then put in a large pan with the butter. Cook over a low heat, stirring, for a few minutes. Add the water then simmer for 45 minutes. Season with salt and white pepper, to taste. Store for 24 hours maximum. Vegetable stock freezes well.

CROUTONS

Makes enough for 4

sunflower or other
    vegetable oil

1 ciabatta loaf, torn into
    bite-size pieces

2 tbsp finely grated
    Parmesan, Grana Padano
    or pecorino cheese

3 sprigs thyme, leaves only,
    finely chopped

½ tsp freshly ground black
    pepper

Useful to have on the table to add to almost all soups – keep these croutons warm in a bowl or basket with a tea towel placed over the top.

Preheat the oven to 180°C/fan 160°C/350°F/Gas 4. Pour enough oil onto the base of a baking tray to coat it thinly then toss the torn bread in it. Scatter over the cheese, thyme and pepper, toss again and bake until golden and crisp, about 15 minutes, turning occasionally. Store in an airtight container and reheat gently before serving.

BEEF BONE MARROW AND BEETROOT SOUP

over new potatoes

Serves 4

Serving dish: individual shallow bowls

For the broth:

450g shin of beef, on the bone

2 beef marrow bones, split or cut into small rounds

1 litre chicken stock (see page 62)

1 onion, halved

1 carrot, halved

1 bay leaf

salt and freshly ground black pepper

4 medium-sized beetroots, washed

1 tbsp balsamic vinegar

1 tbsp vegetable oil

To serve:

4 medium-sized new potatoes, peeled

4 tsp chopped chives

4 tsp sour cream

A nearly authentic version of Russian borscht, with a double-strength broth added to roasted beetroot, served over potatoes and with sour cream on top. This is actually quite a light starter soup, perfect for winter dinners ahead of a roast. The broth can be made a couple of days in advance.

Preheat the oven to 180°C/fan 160°C/350°F/Gas 4. Roast the beef shin and marrow bones together for 45 minutes until well browned. Remove from the oven and put the bones and the chicken stock in a casserole or saucepan. Add the onion, carrot and bay leaf and bring to simmering point. Simmer for 1½ hours or until the meat on the shin is tender.

Season to taste then strain and allow to cool. Refrigerate so that the fat hardens on the surface and can be easily lifted off and discarded. If you make the soup fresh, use a ladle to skim off the fat, removing as much as possible.

The beetroot can be prepared while the beef bones are roasting. Line a baking tray with baking parchment and add the whole beetroots. Add the balsamic vinegar and oil and roll the beetroots around in the tray. Cover with foil and bake at 180°C/fan 160°C/350°F/Gas 4 for 45 minutes, removing the foil for the last 15 minutes. Remove from the oven, allow to cool then peel the beetroots. To finish, put the beetroot and strained meat broth in a liquidiser and process until smooth.

To serve, boil the potatoes until just tender. Cut them in half then slice into bite-size pieces before dividing among the bowls. Reheat the soup then ladle it over the contents of the bowls, scatter with the chives then serve, passing a bowl of sour cream around so that guests can add their own. If you add the sour cream too early, everything in the bowl will bleed into each other and it can look unpleasantly messy – though will taste just as good.

Option: Blended beetroot broth can be eaten chilled as a recherché jelly soup, with sour cream and chives.

CREAMED SQUASH AND APPLE SOUP
with porcini buttered toasts and chestnuts

Serves 4

Serving dish: individual deep bowls

90g butter

2 onions, chopped

2 garlic cloves, chopped

300g cubed butternut
  squash

1 apple, peeled, cored and
  chopped

1.2 litres chicken or
  vegetable stock (see
  page 62)

115g crème fraîche

salt and ground white
  pepper

For the toasts:

4 slices sourdough toast

50g dried porcini, soaked
  in boiling water

4 tbsp softened butter

salt

To serve:

2 tbsp vegetable oil

150g cooked peeled
  chestnuts, chopped into
  'gravel'

red micro leaves or flat-leaf
  parsley (optional)

1 red chilli, finely chopped
  and mixed with 2 tbsp
  olive oil

The colours of autumn in a soup bowl. Butternut squash is ideal for this soup but you can try other types, such as acorn squash or crown prince. If you use pumpkin, it can be a little too sweet so add an extra garlic clove and some lemon juice.

To make the soup, melt the butter in a large pan and add the onions and garlic. Cook over a low heat until soft then add the squash, apple and stock. Bring to the boil and simmer until the squash is tender. Add the crème fraîche then transfer to a liquidiser or food processor/blender. Process until as smooth as possible – always be careful with hot liquid when blending – and then transfer back to the pan. Season with salt and white pepper then set to one side to keep warm while you make the toasts.

Toast or grill one side of the bread slices. Strain the porcini and then blend them with the softened butter. Season with salt and then spread the mushroom mixture over the uncooked surface of the bread slices. Place under the grill and cook until golden and bubbling – about 5–7 minutes. Set aside in a warm place.

Heat the oil in a small pan and fry the chopped chestnuts until golden – cook them gently as they burn easily. Drain on kitchen paper.

To serve the soup, ladle it into bowls and scatter over the chestnuts and micro leaves or parsley (if using). Add a few drops of the chilli oil to each bowl then balance the bread on the side of the bowl. Eat straight away.

Options: Pumpkin (with extra garlic), parsnip or turnip

TOMATO SOUP
over toasted cheese sandwiches

Serves 4

*Serving dish: individual
shallow bowls*

4 tbsp extra virgin olive oil

2–3 garlic cloves, peeled

6 basil leaves

1 x 400g can Italian chopped
  tomatoes

400g ripe baby plum
  tomatoes, halved

300ml chicken or vegetable
  stock (see page 62)

110ml crème fraîche

sea salt and ground white
  pepper

For the sandwiches:

8 slices white farmhouse
  bread

8–12 thin slices Gruyère
  cheese

olive oil, for brushing

To serve:

4 tbsp extra virgin olive
  oil mixed with 3 finely
  chopped basil leaves

A summer soup that is pure pleasure: sweet, simmered tomatoes, with only garlic, stock and a touch of crème fraîche, served with triangles of toasted Gruyère sandwiches. This soup can be served more generously as a main course for lunch or supper.

Put the oil, garlic, basil, canned and fresh tomatoes into a saucepan and bring to simmering point. Simmer for 15 minutes, to sweeten the tomatoes, then add the stock. Bring back to simmering point then remove from the heat. Put in a liquidiser or food processor/blender with the crème fraîche and process until very smooth – always take care when blending hot liquids – then transfer back to the pan.

Make sandwiches with the bread and cheese, then trim off the crusts and brush the outer surfaces with olive oil. Shortly before serving, either bake in the oven at 200°C/fan 180°C/400°F/Gas 6, or toast in a pan until both sides are golden. Keep the sandwiches warm until needed.

To serve, reheat the soup gently without boiling, and season to taste with salt and white pepper. Cut each sandwich into bite-size triangles and divide among the bowls. Pour the soup around the sandwiches and then add a few drops of the basil oil.

WATERCRESS VELVET SOUP
over sautéed black pudding, potato and bacon

Serves 4

Serving dish: pre-warmed
shallow bowls

90g butter

2 onions, chopped

1 garlic clove, chopped

2 medium-sized potatoes
(about 60g peeled
weight), cut into small dice

1.2 litres chicken or
vegetable stock (see
page 62)

3 bunches watercress, tough
stalks removed, finely
chopped (reserve a few
leaves for garnish)

110ml double cream,

salt and ground white
pepper

To serve:

8 rashers dry-cured, smoked
streaky bacon

200g black pudding (type
without pieces of fat)

4–8 small new potatoes,
boiled in their skins until
just tender

The most powerfully flavoured of all green soups, watercress matches perfectly the smoky, slightly salty bacon and mineral flavours in the black pudding – I always feel stronger after eating this soup. To make it into a yet more substantial meal, add a poached egg or a shelled, soft-boiled, five-minute egg.

Melt the butter in a large pan and add the onions and garlic. Cook over a low heat until soft then add the potatoes and stock. Bring to the boil and simmer until the potatoes are tender. Remove from the heat and set aside until 30 minutes before serving (the base can be stored in the fridge for 24 hours).

Gently fry or grill the bacon until it is crisp, then place on kitchen paper to soak up any fat. Allow to cool, then break up the rashers into shards and set aside in a warm place. Remove the skin from the black pudding and crumble into lumps the size of a fingertip. Sauté in a non-stick pan with a little fat. Slice the new potatoes thinly and set aside with the bacon and black pudding.

Within 30 minutes of serving, bring the soup base back to simmering point and add the watercress. Simmer for 1 minute then transfer to a liquidiser or food processor/blender with the double cream. Process until very smooth (always be careful with hot liquid when blending). It is important that the soup is very smooth; if the blender or liquidiser is not powerful enough, put it through a mouli-legumes or food mill, or through a sieve with a wide mesh, to remove any stringy stalk bits from the watercress, so allow extra time for this.

Reheat the soup gently without boiling and season to taste with salt and white pepper. Just before serving, put a mix of the bacon shards, black pudding chunks and potato slices in a heap in the centre of each warmed serving bowl. Pour the soup around the other ingredients. Finally, scatter the reserved watercress leaves around the surface of the soup.

Options: Replace the watercress with wild garlic or spinach, asparagus or fresh peas; try scallops with the bacon in place of the black pudding.

CHICKEN BROTH
with spring vegetables and pistou sauce

Serves: 4

Serving dish: soup bowls

1 tbsp olive oil

1 onion, finely chopped

pinch of dried oregano

2 plum tomatoes, skinned, deseeded and finely chopped, or 1 tsp tomato purée

2 tbsp vermouth (optional)

1 × 400g can white haricot beans, drained

1 medium-sized turnip, peeled and cut into 5mm dice

100g fine green beans, chopped into 1cm pieces

100g peas or broad beans

2 courgettes, cut into 5mm dice

1.2 litres chicken stock (see page 62)

salt and freshly ground black pepper

For the pistou sauce:

6 sprigs basil, leaves only

4 tbsp extra virgin olive oil

1–2 garlic cloves, crushed to a paste with a pinch of salt

2 tbsp freshly grated Parmesan cheese

Green, aromatic and invigorating, this is a soup inspired by the Niçoise soupe au pistou, a simple chicken broth with vegetables and haricot beans, finished with garlic, basil and Parmesan. It is both a beautiful starter soup to eat before the Aïoli Platter on page 226, or before a roast chicken or pork shoulder, and also in a larger quantity as a main dish.

Heat the oil in a large saucepan. Add the onion and cook over a medium-low heat until soft but not coloured. Add the oregano and tomatoes and fry for a minute. Add the vermouth (if using), followed by he beans and all the vegetables and the stock. Bring to simmering point and cook until the vegetables are soft – about 10 minutes. Add salt and pepper to taste.

Put the basil, extra virgin olive oil and garlic into a pestle and mortar or blender and mash to a thick green paste. Stir in the cheese.

To serve the soup, ladle the vegetable broth into bowls, then add a tablespoon of the sauce. It will float in a deliciously fragrant green slick on the surface. Serve with fresh warm baguette or croutons (see page 63).

Option: Add soup pasta to make a substantial supper dish.

MAIN COURSES

MEAT AND FISH

The centrepiece to dinner might
be a great pie with a gasp factor, an
extravagant roast, a simple baked fish or
humble baked pasta dish straight from
the oven and still bubbling. There is no
lack of ideas yet the recipes that are the
best are also those that are practical,
suited to your kitchen, your skills and
also your personality. Our homes are not
restaurants and in them we are cooks,
not chefs. Putting practicality first is
crucial when you choose which main
course to make, but this does not mean
you compromise on creativity.

Ideally, a main course is one to fetch
quickly, place on the table and plate
without too much fuss. If there is
a little bit to fiddle with between a
starter and main course, make sure
the starter is either simple or cold so
you are not cooking throughout the
meal. Ultimately, it is nice to reach
that moment where everything is on
the table and you can sit, breathe and
enjoy yourself in the company of others.
Dishes to prepare in advance and either
rest or keep aside warm are the best for
guest numbers above six.

In some cooking cultures dinner menus
are pared back and – after an appetiser
and bread – a fantastic piece of beef
or fish is eaten on its own with just the
cooking juices or a sauce, then a large
green salad served after. I love this
concept but think many of my guests
would be looking around the table as if
I'd forgotten something – the potatoes.

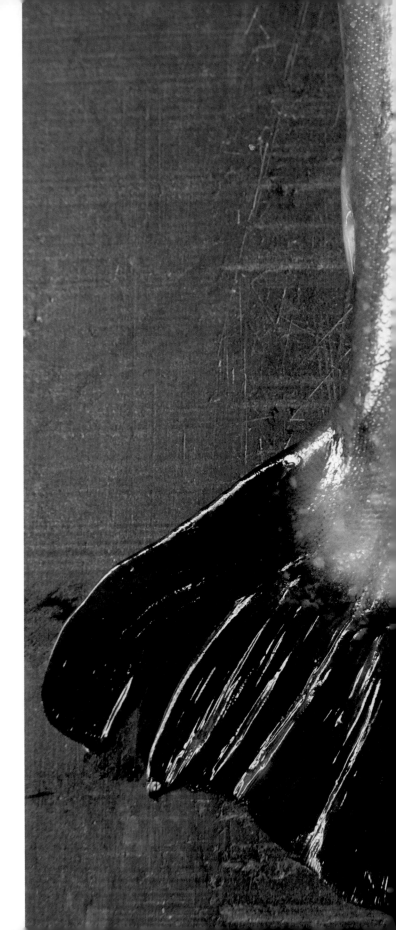

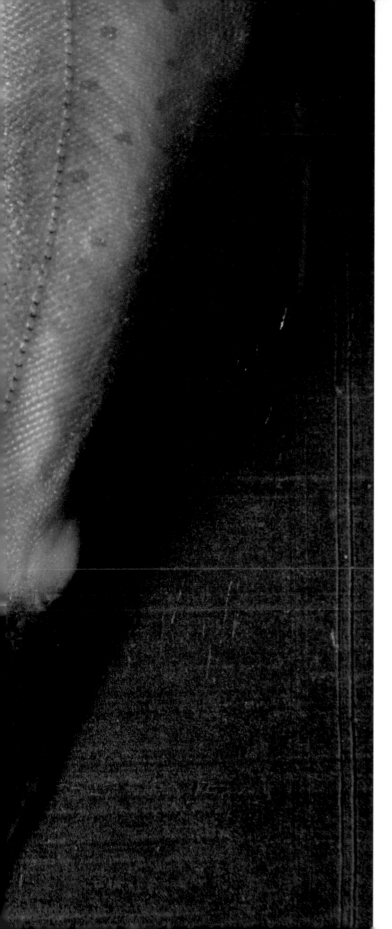

These cuisines teach us, though, that when ingredients are top quality they speak for themselves and there is no need to dress them up heavily with endless vegetable dishes.

The same balance can be achieved on economy. If you splash out on the fish or meat, choose a starter that is modest – a dish of Creamed butter beans with flatbreads (see page 228), for example. You can taste this balance in the food, oddly enough, and it is a significant element of being a good cook. So, too, is sensitivity, to weather and to the seasons. Matching dishes to the season when there is a glut also makes economic sense, as well as being just right for the day. Try to react: so if the summer is unseasonably chilly, a large lemon-scented risotto will warm everyone, for example. This is common-sense, intelligent cooking and very nurturing. I hate rules, except for this: The priority in choosing what to make for dinner is not to think about what you would like, but what your guests would most like to eat.

SIMPLE BAKED WHOLE BRILL
with beurre blanc

Serves: 6–8

Serving dish: individual serving plates

1.3–1.5kg whole brill or other fish (see options, below), gutted and de-scaled
vegetable oil
salt and freshly ground black pepper
a few slices lemon

For the beurre blanc:
4 shallots, chopped
180ml white wine
250g unsalted butter, diced
juice of 1 lemon
sea salt, to taste

To serve:
new potatoes
green salad

A large fresh fish cooked whole is not only a festive spectacle but an easy and unfussy dinner to prepare. When a fish is very fresh and cooked to perfection it needs very little to dress it. In fact, finding that recently landed fish can be more time-consuming than cooking it. Learn to recognise the signs of freshness in fish: look for bright protuberant eyes, red under the gills, shiny, slimy skin and (when the fishmonger and other customers are not looking) prod it to see if it feels cool and firm. Obviously, it should have no smell except that of the sea. Ask the fishmonger to gut the fish and de-scale it if necessary. The head and tail can be removed if your roasting pan is small but it is better to cook the fish whole.

First put the sauce together. Put the shallot and wine in a small pan and simmer until reduced by half. Strain, reserving the liquid, and return it to the pan. Add the butter, let it melt then remove from the heat. To finish the sauce place the pan over a medium heat, let the contents simmer for a minute while you whisk, add the lemon and season with salt. It will emulsify.

Preheat the oven to 180°C/fan 160°C/350°F/Gas 4 and line a large roasting pan with baking parchment. Brush the fish with oil and season, then place in the roasting pan. Put the lemon inside the cavity, bake the fish for about 12 minutes then check it – press the flesh and if your finger makes an indentation, cook for longer. You can also insert the point of a knife and lift it to see if the flesh of the fish easily parts into flakes, right down to the bone. If so, remove it from the oven. Let it rest for a little while with a loose tent of foil on top. It is always better to take the fish out of the oven when you judge it to be a touch undercooked – you will get good at this, with practice, I promise.

To serve the fish, cut away and discard the skin. Cut down the line in the centre and use a spatula to lift portions of the fish onto plates. When the top flesh has gone, lift away the centre bone and head/tail then serve the meat from the underside of the fish. Give the sauce a final whisk, pour a little over each helping and serve, with new potatoes and green salad.

Options: Other whole fish suitable for baking include sea bass, plaice, sea trout, cod and haddock, hake, ray and many other white fish. Turbot, the 'big sister' to bream, is a very beautiful but more extravagant option. Options for sauce: Add 2 tablespoons of grated fresh ginger, with its juice, to the beurre blanc just before serving for a subtly exotic, alternative taste. You can also serve baked fish with hollandaise or mayonnaise (see pages 48 and 221).

CLASSIC FISH PIE

Serves: 6–8

Serving dish: ovenproof dish, approximately 25cm square or circular and 8cm deep

For the base:

1 onion, finely chopped

300g fresh haddock fillet

300g undyed smoked haddock fillet

750ml whole milk

1 bay leaf

small pinch of grated nutmeg

freshly ground black pepper

300g raw king prawns, defrosted and drained on kitchen paper

6 eggs

60g butter

60g plain flour

75ml white wine

300ml double cream

white pepper, to taste

For the mashed potato:

1.4kg floury potatoes (Desiree, Maris Piper, King Edwards,) peeled and cut into chunks

salt

90g butter

1 egg

Good fish pie typifies the practical solution when having people over for a meal. It can be made in advance and if it has to sit in the oven because someone is late, it can do (for a while). Oh, and pretty much everyone loves it. Having said all this, there are tricks to making the ultimate fish pie, one with perfectly cooked fish and oozing sauce underneath, light mashed potato on top with a crisp, nubbly crust. Read on . . .

Put the onion and haddock in a wide shallow pan with the milk, bay leaf, nutmeg and a few grinds of black pepper. Bring to simmering point, cover with a lid or sheet of foil, then simmer for about 5 minutes. Insert a knife into the fillets – which should just about part into flakes but still be transparent inside. Ideally the fish should be a touch underdone before going into the pie so it does not go soft and dry out during baking. Remove from the heat, lift out the fish and leave to cool. Strain the liquid and reserve. Pick the flesh of the haddock away from the skin and remove any bones. Break it into large bite-size pieces and put it in the pie dish. Scatter the raw prawns on the top.

Put the eggs in a pan and cover with water. Bring to the boil and time 4½ minutes. Remove from the heat and run cold water into the pan. Once cool, peel the eggs, cut them in half and put them on top of the fish at the edge of the dish.

In a separate pan, melt the butter over a medium heat, then add the flour and stir to a paste. Whisk in the wine while allowing the sauce to come back to the boil, then begin to whisk in the poaching milk. Do not add it too quickly or the sauce will be lumpy. Bring slowly to the boil, stirring all the time, until it thickens. Add the cream, whisk and leave to cool for 10 minutes – you do not want the hot sauce to overcook the fish. Taste and add a little white pepper. Pour over the fish and eggs and chill for 1 hour until the sauce is set firm.

Preheat the oven to 200°C/fan 180°C/400°F/Gas 6. Boil the potatoes in salted water until soft and drain well. Mash with the butter then beat in the egg. Season to taste with salt. Spread the mash evenly over the fish mixture. Scratch the surface with a fork and bake for 35–45 minutes, until the pie is bubbling and the surface is nicely browned.

POACHED SALMON

with hollandaise

Serves: 6–8

Serving dish: large oval serving platter

1.5–1.8kg whole salmon, gutted and de-scaled

salt and freshly ground black pepper

a few slices lemon

1 quantity Hollandaise (see page 48)

For the poaching liquid:

1–1.5 litres water

2 carrots, roughly chopped

1 celery stick, roughly chopped

1 onion, roughly chopped

1 bay leaf

4 cloves

6 peppercorns

75ml white wine vinegar

100ml white wine

To serve cold salmon:

1 cucumber, deseeded and part peeled, shaved into ribbons

small-leaf herbs, micro leaves, fennel fronds

extra virgin olive oil

lemons, quartered or halved, then grilled

1 quantity Mayonnaise (see page 221)

At its best, when perfectly poached, slightly pink in the centre and the tender fish itself the best quality, with little fat and a clear, authentic flavour, salmon is a very special dish for dinner. It lost its reputation, though, becoming a buffet-table cliché; a fatty, intensively reared creature served dry from overcooking alongside bottled sauces. Yet there is a time for a proper poached salmon, when numbers and appetites are unpredictable and everyone has to help themselves. It is a matter of taking more care, and serving good leafy salads, buttery potatoes and a real hollandaise. You will be surprised at how many people tell you they have never tasted salmon like this before.

Prepare the fish by seasoning the cavity and inserting the lemon slices. Put the poaching liquid ingredients in a fish kettle and bring to the boil. Simmer for 20 minutes then lower in the fish. Immediately turn off the heat, and wait 15–20 minutes depending on the size of the fish. Alternatively, you can wrap the fish in buttered foil or baking parchment, then bake in the oven at 180°C/400°F/Gas 6. The fish is cooked when it feels firm and springy to the touch, about 20–25 minutes. Be careful not to overcook it.

Either eat warm, with the hollandaise, or allow to cool, for cold salmon. It can be stored in the fridge for several hours before serving. To present a cold salmon, remove all the skin from the body. Dress the cucumber ribbons and herbs with olive oil, then strew all over the salmon.

Options: Sea trout, arctic char, sea bass.

POACHED ARCTIC CHAR

with soy, ginger and spring onions

Serves: 6–8

Serving dish: large platter

1.3–1.5kg whole arctic char or other fish (see options, below), gutted and de-scaled

For the broth:

400ml light soy sauce

300ml water

300ml Fino sherry

bunch spring onions, green part only, chopped

9cm piece fresh ginger, peeled and sliced very thin

salt, to taste

As with the baked bream, a whole poached fish adds a sense of occasion to a dinner, even though it's very quick and easy to do. The Chinese and Southeast Asian way of poaching fish is light and clean, perfect for a healthy midweek dinner. All it needs is a side dish of plain rice and perhaps some steamed pak choi, choy sum and/or green beans.

I have used arctic char in my recipe. This is a white-fleshed member of the salmon family which is farmed in the UK – coincidentally in the old spring-water-fed watercress beds in our village. You can, however, use salmon, sea trout or large rainbow trout. Sea bass is also suitable. The sauce is a mildly spicy ginger, sherry and spring onion broth. For a large fish, you will need a fish kettle. If you do not have one, some fishmongers will lend them. Alternatively, buy smaller fish or the joint of a fish – i.e. without head, or just the tail end – and steam it in a roasting pan covered with foil.

Put all the broth ingredients in the fish kettle and bring to the boil. Taste and add a little salt if you feel the broth needs it. Lower the fish into the kettle – it will have a loose metal lining which helps you do this. Let the liquid come back to the boil then remove from the heat, cover with the lid and leave for 10 minutes. Check the fish – press with your finger to see if it is firm. It is now ready to serve – but can sit in the warm liquid for 15 minutes or so. Lift it out and place it on the serving platter – it will look beautiful. Serve at the table.

Options: Use salmon, sea trout, sea bass or rainbow trout in place of char.

PIGEON BREASTS

with figs and parsley pearl barley

Serves: 6–8

Serving dish: medium platter or board

2 tbsp melted butter

16 pigeon breasts

8 figs, halved

sea salt and freshly ground
   black pepper

For the parsley pearl barley:

400g pearl barley

2 tbsp butter

4 shallots, chopped

½ tsp of ground allspice

8 tbsp finely chopped flat-
   leaf parsley

3 tbsp lemon juice

5 tbsp extra virgin olive oil

salt, to taste

Dark ruby and medium rare, the gently gamey, savoury flavour of pigeon matches the sweetness of autumn figs exquisitely. Inexpensive pigeon is conveniently quick to prepare and very successful if you follow the simple rule of resting it well before serving.

First make the parsley pearl barley: put the barley in a saucepan with 1.5 litres of water and heat until simmering. Simmer for about 20–30 minutes until the barley is cooked through, but not fluffy. Drain and set to one side. Melt the butter in a frying pan and add the shallots. Sauté until soft then add the allspice and pearl barley. Remove from the heat.

Next, cook the pigeon. Place a pan ona a high heat and add the butter. Season the pigeon breasts with salt and pepper. Quickly fry the pigeon breasts for 30 seconds each side. Remove from the pan and set aside in a warm place covered by a loose tent of foil, for 10 minutes.

Meanwhile, lower the heat in the pan and fry the fig halves, cut side down, for about 1 minute. Remove from the pan and set aside with the pigeon.

Finish the pearl barley by adding the parsley, lemon juice and olive oil. Season with salt to taste. Cut the rested pigeon breasts across the grain, into 5mm pieces. To serve, spread the barley all over the platter, then heap the sliced pigeon and figs on top.

Options: Duck, mallard, pheasant or partridge breasts.

PORK AND COCKLES
with samphire and lettuce

Serves: 6–8

Serving dish: large shallow pan or deep platter

1kg cockles

2 tbsp chopped rosemary leaves

1 tbsp chopped sage leaves

1 tbsp thyme leaves

2 garlic cloves, chopped and mashed to a paste with salt

4 tbsp olive oil

1.5–2kg boned and rolled leg of pork, without crackling or fat layer

1 tbsp butter

2 shallots, chopped

250ml cider

200g samphire, woody stems trimmed off

1 butterhead lettuce, leaves only, stalks removed and torn

To serve:

boiled new potatoes or egg pappardelle (wide flat noodles.)

Now and again when you have a group of people to dinner who you know enjoy something slightly left field, you can challenge their palates with a dish that appears to break the rules. Meat with fish? Well, it is not so unusual. Anchovies are often used as seasoning for lamb or pork and scallops go beautifully with bacon. Cockles, which are raked out of the sand on British beaches, are salty and sweet at the same time and lend their flavour notes nicely to the rich flavour of marinated roast pork. I have added samphire for salinity, which is easy to buy, but also lettuce to this dish as sea lettuce can be hard to source. English butterhead lettuce makes an adequate alternative.

Discard any cockles that are cracked. Rinse under the cold tap then store for 45–60 minutes in salted water. They usually contain sand and this should sink to the bottom of the container. Mix together the herbs, garlic and olive oil and rub all over the pork. Leave it to marinate for a minimum of 1 hour, or overnight.

Preheat the oven to 200°C/fan 180°C/400°F/Gas 6. Put the pork in a shallow pan and roast for 15 minutes. Turn the oven down to 160°C/fan 140°C/325°F/Gas 3 and continue to cook for 1–1¼ hours. The pork is done when the juices inside run clear if a skewer is inserted. Set aside to rest in a warm place, covered with foil, for 20 minutes.

Melt the butter in a large pan and add the shallots. Cook until transparent, then add the cider. Lift the cockles carefully out of their bath of water, leaving any sandy sediment behind; add them to the pan then cover with a lid to steam. Cook for 3–4 minutes until all the cockles are open – throw away any that remain shut. Scoop out the cockles with a slotted spoon into a bowl, then pass the juice in the pan through a sieve to remove any remaining sand or sediment. Clean the pan, add back the clear juice and cockles, plus the samphire and lettuce. Cover and gently heat until the 'sea vegetables' soften – about 1–2 minutes. Remove from the heat.

To serve, slice the pork and add it to the pan, tucking it in between the cockles and vegetables, but not submerging it in the juice – so that it stays tender.

GUINEA FOWL, CHICKEN AND LEEK PIE

Serves: 6–8

Serving dish: 3.5–4-litre deep ovenproof dish

1 1.5kg free-range chicken

1 1.3kg free-range guinea fowl

sea salt and freshly ground black pepper

60g butter

1.5 litres chicken stock (see page 62)

4 leeks, cut into rounds and washed

6 sprigs tarragon, leaves only

300ml double cream

For the pastry:

300g self-raising flour, plus extra for dusting

150g beef suet

½ tsp sea salt

water, to mix

1 egg, beaten with a pinch of salt and 1 tbsp water, to glaze

To serve:

boiled potatoes

knob of butter

It is much easier to prepare than it perhaps looks. A marrow bone makes a good pie chimney but you can use a regular one, or even an upturned egg cup. Suet pastry is very easy to make and handle, and becomes crisp as pork crackling the longer it cooks. I leave the meat on the joints, but you can take all off the bone if using a smaller dish.

Joint the chicken and the guinea fowl into eight pieces each. Cut off the legs and then through the joint to separate the drumsticks from thighs. Cut off the wings, with half of the breast meat attached. Then fillet the rest of the breast meat off the carcass. Season all with salt and pepper.

Melt the butter in a large casserole dish and brown the chicken and guinea fowl joints in batches. Put all in the casserole, followed by the the stock. Bring to the boil then turn down to a simmer and cook for 45 minutes, slowly bubbling, until the meat becomes quite tender.

Remove from the heat and take out the meat joints, transferring them to a large pie dish with a pie chimney in the centre. You can take the meat off the bone at this point if you want to, or if you do not have a large enough pie dish. Scatter over the leeks and tarragon. Simmer the stock in the casserole for 15 minutes to reduce it a little. Then stir in the cream and seasoning. Pour this over the chicken in the pie dish, leaving at least 4cm clear at the top so it does not bubble over, and allow to cool while you make and roll the pastry.

Preheat the oven to 190°C/fan 170°C/375°F/Gas 5. Put the flour and suet in a large bowl with the salt, mix briefly and add a little water at a time, pushing the pastry together with your hands, until you have a dry dough.

Dust the worktop with flour and then roll out the pastry until it is 5mm thick and much larger than the surface area of the pie dish. Wet the edge of the dish with water and lay the pastry over the top. Trim the pastry, leaving about 5cm hanging down the side of the dish. Cut a small 'x' in the centre so the pie chimney pokes through. Bake for about 40 minutes until deep golden and very crisp. Serve immediately, with boiled buttered potatoes.

COQ AU VIN

Serves: 6–8

Serving dish: large oval platter

For the starting broth:

1 bottle red wine (choose an inexpensive French Merlot or Pinot Noir)

300ml chicken stock

2 bay leaves

1 garlic clove, crushed

400g button mushrooms

For the chicken:

120g unsmoked lardons

2 tbsp duck fat

8 small pickling onions, peeled and left whole

3–3.5kg chicken, jointed into 6–8 pieces and seasoned

90ml brandy

3 garlic cloves, peeled and left whole

1 bundle of herbs, with a carrot, all tied together

For the roux, to thicken:

1 tbsp butter

1 tbsp plain flour

To serve:

croutons (see page 63)

Pommes purée (see page 120)

This is the definitive chicken casserole, ideal to prepare on a leisurely autumn or winter weekend for guests who have big appetites and treasure good wine. Serve it with the smoothest mashed potatoes, 'pommes purée' (see page 120), and begin with a crisp and light vegetable starter. Don't use bad wine, because you will be able to taste it. A simple bottle of decent French table wine is best. Also, buy a large free-range, corn-fed chicken which retains its texture after a slow simmer.

Put the wine, stock, bay leaves and garlic in large saucepan and bring to simmering point. Simmer for 20 minutes to reduce the liquid and thicken it slightly. After 15 minutes, add the mushrooms. Strain, set aside the mushrooms, and keep the liquid ready to add after cooking the chicken. In a large, heavy-based casserole fry the lardons in a little of the duck fat, then scoop them out of the pan and set aside. Fry the onions briefly until they colour, then remove and set aside with the lardons.

Brown the chicken pieces in the remaining fat until golden on all sides. Turn down the heat and add the brandy – it might flame but it will die down. Ideally, you should set it alight, but if this is not for you just let it simmer at a low heat for 1 minute. Add the lardons and onions back to the casserole with the simmered wine, the whole garlic cloves and the bouquet of herbs. Bring to simmering point then cover and cook very slowly for 40 minutes, by which time the meat will be tender. Use a slotted spoon to lift out the cooked chicken pieces, lardons and mushrooms. Pick out and discard the garlic and bouquet. Put the chicken in a low oven to keep warm, covered with a loose piece of foil.

Boil the liquid for 10 minutes to reduce it more. Add the mushrooms and cook for 5 minutes. In a small saucepan, melt the butter with the flour and cook until it becomes pale and sandy-coloured. Add this to the liquid, but do not stir it. Bring the liquid back to the boil, let it simmer for just a minute then turn it off and stir it – it will thicken to the texture of single cream. If too thick, add a little stock or water to thin it. When ready to eat, pour the hot thickened wine sauce over the chicken and serve straight away, with croutons and pommes purée.

CASSOULET

Serves: 8–10

Serving dish: large casserole

1kg dried white haricot
   beans, soaked
   overnight in water

1 × 250g bacon 'chop'

8 × 1cm-thick slices lean
   pork shoulder meat,
   off the bone

2 tbsp goose fat

800g Toulouse sausages
   (garlic and herb
   seasoning)

1 carrot, finely diced

2 onions, finely diced

250g canned chopped
   tomatoes

1.5 litres chicken stock

4 confit duck legs

1 onion, studded with 2
   cloves

1 bay leaf tied with a
   small bunch each of
   parsley and thyme

3 garlic cloves, crushed

sea salt and freshly
   ground black pepper

To serve:

250g sourdough bread,
   torn into small pieces

vegetable oil, for frying

Cassoulet is a very rewarding recipe to make, needing patience rather than skill to build its various parts. When it has all come together, however, it is a very practical dish to serve to a large number. Its 'one-pot' character leaves you with very little to do at dinner, apart from provide a good green salad to eat after, with cheese and/or a pudding.

A word about timing: the beans can be simmered at the same time as the pork and sausages. Drain the beans, put them in a large pan, add water and bring to the boil. Skim any foam off the top and add the bacon chop. Simmer for at least 1 hour, or until the beans are just tender – do not overcook them. Leave to sit in the cooking liquid until needed.

Meanwhile, fry the pork shoulder slices in the duck fat, just browning each side – they do not need to cook through. Add the sausages and briefly brown all over. Add the carrot and diced onions, cook for a few minutes then add the tomatoes. Cover with the stock, keeping a surplus, and simmer for 45 minutes.

Preheat the oven to 150°C/fan 130°C/300°F/Gas 2. Put the confit duck legs into a pan and turn them over a medium heat to remove the fat. Separate the thigh from the drumsticks, or take the meat off the bone. Drain the beans, reserving the liquid. Remove and discard the rind from the bacon, and chop the meat. Put it in the casserole then begin to add all the meats and beans, distributing them well. Add all the stock, and use the bean water to top up if necessary. Submerge the whole onion, the herbs, garlic and seasoning. Put the lid on the casserole and bake for about 1–1¼ hours. All should steam together and the flavours combine.

In the meantime, fry the bread in the oil, until golden. Take the casserole out of the oven and remove the onion and the herb bundle. Scatter the fried bread over the surface and serve.

Options: Confit pheasant, chicken or goose – in place of duck. Including pork meat is optional.

GAME RAGÙ
with egg pasta

Serves: 6–8

Serving dish: large platter

2kg diced mixed game
4–5 tbsp olive oil
4 onions, finely chopped
3 celery sticks, strings pared
   off and finely chopped
2 heaped tbsp tomato purée
1 litre chicken stock (see
   page 62) or beef stock
1 bay leaf
2 small sprigs rosemary
salt and freshly ground black
   pepper
250–300g dried egg
   pappardelle or other
   dried egg ribbon pasta

For the marinade:
300ml red wine
1 tsp freshly ground black
   pepper
1 tsp finely chopped
   rosemary leaves
6 juniper berries, crushed
2 tbsp extra virgin olive oil
juice of ½ lemon

To serve:
4 tbsp chopped flat-leaf
   parsley
4 tbsp shaved pecorino
   cheese

A notch above Bolognese, this is a rich, deep-flavoured stew-sauce to dress wide ribbons of egg pasta and model fare for wild meat enthusiasts. You can buy diced mixed game from butchers (see Directory, page 269), which should include venison, rabbit, pigeon and some game-bird meat, too. I also use this recipe to make faux 'wild boar' ragu, using diced shoulder of pork and adding extra juniper to the marinade.

Ideally, the meat needs to be cut small, about 1cm dice, so cut it smaller if necessary. Put the meat and the marinade ingredients into a non-corrosive bowl, mix well and leave for at least 4 hours. Place a sieve over a bowl, tip the meat into it and set to one side. Put the marinade juices into a saucepan and simmer for about 10 minutes until reduced by half. Set this aside, too.

To prepare the ragù, put the oil in a large frying pan over a medium heat and gently sauté the onions and celery until they are soft and transparent. Use a slotted spoon to transfer to a plate. Brown the meat in the pan, in batches, transferring each batch to the plate with the onion mixture. When all is done, put everything back in the pan and add the reduced wine marinade. Cook for 1 minute then add the tomato purée. Cook for a further minute, then add the stock and herbs and simmer for about 1½–2 hours, over a very low heat, until the meat is tender. Alternatively, you can cook the ragù overnight, in a casserole in the oven, at 70-80°C. Season with salt and pepper, then keep the ragù warm while you cook the pasta.

Put at least 3 litres of water into a pan, add a tablespoon of salt and, while it is boiling fast, add the pasta. Follow the cooking time on the packet – and when the pasta is tender, drain it, reserving a couple of tablespoons of the cooking liquid. Add the pasta to the ragù along with the reserved cooking liquid and simmer for a minute. Serve, scattering the parsley over and handing round the cheese.

RARE ROAST SIRLOIN OF BEEF AND SAUCES

For a treat, the immeasurably deep flavour of well-hung sirloin cannot be touched if roasted perfectly and served with the right sauce for the season, or that to match other dishes. It is a good meal for planning ahead, because you can roast the meat an hour before sitting down, test it then rest it in a warm place. It is nice eaten warm as opposed to hot, it will retain its heat and the texture will also benefit as the cooked meat relaxes. Sirloin is not a cheap cut of beef but there is very little wastage at all and you can get a lot of helpings out of a large 2kg piece.

Successfully roasting a whole boneless piece of beef will come down to good judgement. You can put your trust in a meat thermometer, but, if so, invest in a good one because the difference between perfectly done beef and ruin is a matter of a few degrees. I have made that expensive mistake and now always use a natural test as well – see opposite.

Every cut of beef will vary, so this recipe is set out to help guide you. Just keep testing carefully and you will become an expert beef cook.

TRIMMING AND FAT:

For ease, I ask the butcher to trim a boned cut of sirloin but not to roll and tie it. I love brown and bubbly edges of fat but have come to the conclusion that it is for the Sunday roast with Yorkshire pudding, and not right for dinner with sauces. Before you roast, rub a little olive oil, dripping or butter all over the meat.

SEASONING:

Plenty of freshly ground black pepper, some sea salt and (optional) a few thyme leaves and fennel seeds.

OVEN SETTING:

Electric ovens – use the fan with grill setting, sometimes called turbo grill. Check the handbook to make sure.

UNCOOKED TEMPERATURE:

Remove the cut from the refrigerator 1 hour before roasting and store at room temperature.

Trimmed, boned sirloin or rump – approximate cooking times at 160°C/fan 140°C/325°F/Gas 3:

Test meat a few minutes in advance of timing below.

Always set the oven to 200°C/fan 180°C/400°F/Gas 6 and turn down 5–10 minutes after cooking begins.

1kg cut	Serves 4–6	30 minutes
1.5kg cut	Serves 6–8	45 minutes
2kg cut	Serves 8–10	65 minutes

COOKED BEEF TEMPERATURES FOR RARE BEEF:

Rare	(cool, deep red centre)	51°C/124°F
Medium rare	(warm, deep red centre)	57°C/134.5°F

TO SUCCESSFULLY TEST NATURALLY:

- A few minutes before the estimated cooking time, insert a metal skewer into the centre of the beef. Leave it for 30–60 seconds then remove it.
- If the part of the skewer in contact with the centre of the meat is cold the beef is underdone.
- If cool, the meat is rare.
- If warm, it is medium rare.
- You can test meat as often as you wish, taking into account that the oven will lose heat if the door is opened often.

RESTING:

Cover with a loose tent of foil and rest at warm room temperature, about 16–18°C/61–64.5°F. Rest for a minimum of 15 minutes, and up to 1 hour before serving. The meat will rise in temperature by a degree as it relaxes.

Squeeze a little lemon juice over the roast before carving.

CARVING:

Cut 5–7.5mm slices across the grain of the meat. Serve on warm plates – not hot.

ALTERNATIVE CUTS TO SERVE RARE

FILLET OF BEEF:

Set the oven to 190°C/fan 170°C/375°F/Gas 5 and turn down 5 minutes after cooking begins.

Whole (2–3kg)	Serves 12–16	Roast for 20 minutes at 160°C/fan 140°C/325°F/Gas 3
Half (1–1.5kg)	Serves 6–10	Roast for 35 minutes at 160°C/fan 140°C/325°F/Gas 3

Instructions for resting and carving: as above. Serve on warm plates – not hot.

SMALL CHEAP CUTS:

Lean cuts like top rump (sometimes called picayune), onglet (feather or hanger steak) and skirt steak (bavette) are best if cooked for 1 minute each side on the hob in a grill pan, then transferred to a 160°C/fan 140°C/325°F/Gas 3 oven for a few minutes – then test inner temperature. A reliable visible indication of doneness is to look for red droplets appearing on the surface of the meat – indicating medium rare.

Remove from the oven and rest for a good 15 minutes in a warm place, lightly covered with a sheet of foil. Squeeze a little lemon juice over the roast before carving. These cuts must be cut into 5mm slices because they are tougher than prime cuts. Serve on warm plates – not hot.

SAUCES TO SERVE WITH RARE ROASTED BEEF

1. BÉARNAISE SAUCE

Serves: 6–8

1 large or 4 small shallots, chopped

225g unsalted butter

1 tsp ground mixed pepper (black, white and pink)

90ml white wine vinegar

90ml dry white wine

6 egg yolks

salt and ground white pepper

1 sprig tarragon, chopped

juice of ½ lemon

Beautiful tarragon and shallot-tinted, buttery sauce – the most indulgent of all, especially with fried potatoes or boiled new potatoes on the side. Like the hollandaise on page 48, you can make béarnaise up to two hours in advance and store it in a wide-necked Thermos.

Put the shallots in a pan and fry them in a small knob of the butter. Add the mixed pepper, vinegar and wine and simmer until you have approximately 3 tablespoons. Strain through a tea strainer and set the liquid to one side. Melt the remaining butter and keep it warm.

Put the egg yolks in a mixing bowl with 1 tablespoon of water. Whisk the eggs until foamy and larger in volume – an electric hand whisk is ideal. Add the wine-vinegar reduced liquid and whisk again.

Slowly add the warm melted butter to the egg mixture, whisking continuously. When all the butter has been incorporated, place the bowl over a pan of hot, barely simmering water, and whisk it slowly (by hand is best) until the sauce thickens. It should coat the back of a spoon thickly. Taste the sauce and season with salt and white pepper, add the tarragon and lemon juice, give one final whisk and serve – or store it.

Option: Replace the tarragon with chives. Peppery and fresh-flavoured, this is a pretty pink and green summer sauce for beef. If the radish leaves are in good condition, use some in place of the rocket for an extra kick.

2. HORSERADISH, ROCKET AND RADISH SALSA

Serves: 6–8

3 tbsp grated fresh
  horseradish
2 tbsp lemon juice
2 tbsp small capers
2 tbsp cornichons, sliced
1 large bunch radishes
  (about 30), thinly sliced
100g (1 large bunch) wild
  rocket, chopped
1 tbsp chopped chives
1 tsp freshly ground black
  pepper
150ml extra virgin olive oil

There is a symbiosis in putting members of the radish family together, a pretty and punchy clash of peppery flavours that works well for springtime-summer steak dinners.

Mix all the ingredients together and season with salt if necessary. Serve in a bowl beside the beef.

4. LEMON AND ESPELETTE PEPPER BUTTER

Serves: 6–8

180g salted butter, soft
3 tsp Espelette pepper
3 tbsp very finely chopped
  curly parsley
2 tsp grated lemon zest

For steak dinners with a Basque theme – serve this sauce seasoned with fruity, mildly hot chilli powder from the coastal hinterland near the French–Spanish border. This is great with the humble cuts – onglet and bavette – and fried cubes of potato dressed with aïoli (see page 226) on the side.

Mix all the ingredients together in a bowl then scoop out and place on a board. Form into a rough sausage shape and then wrap like a cracker. Refrigerate, then, when you serve slices of the beef, place a small slice of butter on top so that it melts over the meat.

3. LIME, FRIED MINT AND CHILLI SALSA

Serves: 6–8

8 small sprigs mint, leaves
  only
4 tbsp groundnut oil
juice of 4 limes
4 tbsp maple syrup, or more
2 tbsp Shaoxing rice wine
2 tsp Chinese red vinegar or
  rice vinegar
4 tbsp light soy sauce
4 spring onions, green part
  only, chopped
1–2 tsp chilli bean paste, or
  to taste

A very light and tangy sauce for those days off richness. Add to the beef at the last minute, once carved and served, or the lime juice will 'cook' the meat.

Fry the mint leaves in the oil over a medium heat for a few seconds, then scoop out with a slotted spoon and drain on kitchen paper. Set aside.

Mix the lime juice with the maple syrup, then add more of the syrup if it is too acidic. Add the remaining ingredients, then stir in the mint and it is ready to serve.

5. TAGLIATA

Serves: 6–8

200g mature pecorino
  cheese
300g rocket leaves
8 tbsp extra virgin olive oil
sea salt

In Tuscany the local beef (Chianina, Maremmana, Pisana) is eaten rare, sliced, with shavings of the region's pecorino cheese, extra virgin olive oil and wild rocket. These flavours, combined with the flavour of the red meat and its juices, are especially delicious and so suitable for summer dinners.

Shave the pecorino thinly using a potato peeler or mandolin then set it aside in a bowl. When the beef has been cooked, rested and sliced, put it on a large board or individual plates and scatter over the rocket and pecorino. Zigzag over some olive oil, scatter with salt and eat immediately.

PASTA, RICE, VEGETABLE

Big, comforting main courses were a frequent feature of my own early supper parties. Choosing to cook big pools of glowing risotto, succulent baked dishes of tubular pasta with crispy tops or heady, fragrant biryanis had a lot to do with cost. I might have roasted a chicken for friends but never an expensive joint of beef or rack of lamb. Pasta and rice dishes made sense. Everyone loved them.

My mother had given me an illustrated copy of Elizabeth David's *Italian Food* for a birthday or Christmas, I forget which, and from it I learned to make a real risotto, adding homemade chicken stock to it slowly until the rice was cooked just right. At that time, in the late eighties, Italian dinners were still very much 'spag bol' or chicken Milanese, so for me there was much to discover about authentic regional Italian cooking. It was exciting to make real ricotta gnocchi or a proper ragù, and my friends were wonderfully appreciative, if occasionally necessarily sympathetic, guinea pigs.

The following recipes are dedicated to the memories of that time, and also to a new generation of supper cooks. Over to you – among them are some of my favourites. They are just right for dinner party novices, as they are for old hands. I still reference these recipes, and variations of them, all the time.

Vegetarian meals are no longer considered 'strange'. Modern manners mean we must ask invited guests if there is anything they do not eat. My parents' generation could be hard-nosed about dietary requirements; the sole vegetarian coming to Sunday lunch had to make do with eating the roast potatoes and waiting for the cheese course. They suffered in silence, which is not something anyone wants today. If you have guests coming to dinner who do not eat meat or fish, give their food as much attention as you would for anyone. It can also be a nice gesture to make extra, because it is often the case that the meat-eaters look enviously at the vegetable dish. This way, vegetarian guests will not feel singled out.

Included also in this section are smaller, basic vegetable dishes. These can be offered as side dishes to meat or fish main courses, or expanded to add to a vegetable-only menu (see Garden Party, page 208).

LEMON RISOTTO
with rocket and rocket flowers

Serves: 6

Serving dish: large shallow pan

2 tbsp butter, plus extra to finish the cooking

1 onion, very finely chopped

180g risotto rice (carnaroli or arborio)

100ml white wine

1.5 litres chicken or vegetable stock (see page 62), simmering in a pan

120g freshly grated Grana Padano, Parmesan or pecorino cheese

zest and juice of 2 lemons

sea salt and ground white pepper

To serve:

4 handfuls of wild rocket and flowers, if available

I love this stimulating risotto, with or before a fish course, or with salads on a warm evening. I have included rocket flowers in the recipe, perhaps just to illustrate the rightness of this recipe for early summer, when including a flower petal as decoration, a totally frivolous addition, puts the dish in the context of the season. If you grow rocket, the white flowers with fine dark veins will appear when the plant 'bolts'. White or yellow violas and marigold petals can also be used but, if not available, do not let it put you off making the risotto.

Melt the butter in a large shallow pan and add the onion. Cook gently over a medium-low heat until soft, but not coloured. Add the rice and sauté it gently for 2 minutes, stirring. Add the wine and let it bubble. It will be absorbed into the rice.

Keeping the temperature of the pan medium-low, add 2 ladlefuls of the simmering stock to the pan. Let it bubble and become absorbed, then add more stock. Continue like this until the rice swells and slowly cooks while more and more stock is absorbed.

After about 20–25 minutes bite into a grain of rice or cut it – if it is still raw in the centre, continue adding stock and cooking. When the raw centre is just a speck of opaque white, add a little stock – so the risotto has a soupy consistency – then add half the cheese and another tablespoonful of butter, followed by the lemon zest and juice. Turn off the heat – the lemon does not benefit by further cooking and needs to taste really fresh. Season with salt and pepper, to taste, then scatter over the rocket and flowers, then serve. Hand round the remaining cheese.

VEGETABLE BIRYANI

with coconut baked under a pie crust

Serves: 6–8

Serving dish: large pie dish or casserole

250g basmati rice

2 tbsp yellow split peas or pigeon peas

125ml vegetable oil

4 garlic cloves, crushed

6cm piece fresh ginger, peeled and grated

4 onions, chopped

6 cardamom pods

3 cloves

1 tsp ground turmeric

¼ tsp asafoetida

4 tomatoes, chopped

4 tbsp plain yoghurt

2 tbsp desiccated coconut

sea salt, to taste

8 green chillies, cut lengthways into slivers

2 potatoes, unpeeled, cut into thin sticks

½ cauliflower, cut into small sliced florets

3cm cinnamon stick

plain flour, for dusting

300g ready-made shortcrust pastry

For the green chutney:

6 tbsp plain Greek yoghurt

4 tbsp chopped fresh coriander leaves

1 tsp sugar

When dinner necessitates something vegetable-based with many levels of flavour, an authentic biryani cooked under a pastry crust combines festivity with solace. The purpose of the crust is not for eating necessarily, but to create a unique chamber for the ingredients underneath, absorbing excess steam from the spiced rice and vegetables while remaining airtight. You can take the crust off before serving, to avoid confusion, and then serve the biryani alongside a bowl of fresh yoghurt, green chilli and coriander chutney. This is a very filling and rich rice dish, great for vegetarian suppers, but it could also be served alongside the spiced barbecued poussins on page 190.

Preheat the oven to 180°C/fan 160°C/350°F/Gas 4.

Put the rice and peas in a saucepan, cover with at least 5cm of water and bring to the boil. Simmer for 10–13 minutes until the rice is cooked al dente, with just a bit of bite to it. Drain into a sieve then spread out on a plate and set aside to cool.

Meanwhile, heat half the oil in a wide frying pan, add the garlic, ginger and onions and fry until golden brown. Add the cardamoms, cloves and turmeric, followed by the asafoetida and tomatoes. Finally, stir in the yoghurt and coconut and cook for a few minutes – you will have a thick and creamy sauce. Season with salt to taste and set aside.

Heat the remaining oil in another pan. Add the chillies and vegetables and stir-fry until the vegetables are part-cooked. Now combine everything and transfer to the casserole or pie dish. Place the cinnamon stick on top.

Dust the worktop with flour and roll out the pastry into a disc larger than the surface of the dish. Brush the edge of the dish with water and drape the pastry over the top. Bake for 40 minutes.

1 tsp cumin seeds

2 green chillies, halved and deseeded

For the date-tamarind chutney:

100g dates, pitted

100ml tamarind pulp

50ml water

½ tsp garam masala

To serve:

4 tbsp chopped fresh coriander leaves

1 lime, cut into 6 wedges

While the biryani finishes cooking, prepare the chutneys. Blend all the green chutney ingredients together in a liquidiser then put in a bowl. Put the dates and tamarind in a small saucepan with the water and garam masala and cook for about 5 minutes, until the dates soften. Liquidise until smooth then put in a bowl.

To serve the biryani, remove the pie crust, then scatter over the fresh coriander leaves. Put it on the table with the bowls of chutney and the lime wedges.

BAKED PENNE

with chopped beef, pancetta and chicken livers

Serves: 6–8

Serving dish: 4-litre ovenproof dish, 5–7cm deep

For the ragù:

4 tbsp vegetable oil

2 onions, finely chopped

2 carrots, finely chopped

1 celery stick, finely chopped

4 garlic cloves, chopped

250g thin-cut pancetta, cut into small pieces

250g chicken livers, finely chopped

1.5kg chuck steak, chopped small, or lean beef mince

1 tsp dried oregano

1 tsp chopped rosemary leaves

1 bay leaf

200ml white wine

100ml tomato purée

2 litres beef stock, plus extra to top up

90g butter

1 tsp ground black pepper

sea salt, to taste

For the cheese sauce:

750ml whole milk

a few gratings of nutmeg

1 bay leaf

50g butter

50g plain flour

100g freshly grated Parmesan cheese

With a proper, slow-cooked sauce made with chopped beef, pancetta and finely chopped chicken livers, this pasta bake will feed a lot at little expense. Perhaps the only cost is your patience. Make the ragù the day or evening before your supper party. It takes about 45 minutes to get it to the slow-simmering phase. For the next few hours you need do nothing at all except give it a little stir now and again, while the meat tenderises. Even better, if you have a warming oven with a temperature of 70–80°C/158–176°F, like the bottom oven of an Aga, the sauce will cook beautifully if left overnight.

To make the ragù, heat half the oil in a large casserole and add the vegetables and garlic. Sauté until soft but not coloured then remove from the pan and set to one side. Add a little more oil and fry the pancetta until crisp, then remove and set aside. Add the chicken livers and stir-fry only briefly. Set aside with the pancetta.

Fry the chopped or minced beef in batches, using a little extra oil. Fry it over quite a high heat, to colour it. When all the beef has been browned, add back the pancetta, chicken livers and vegetables. Add the herbs and wine and let the mixture bubble for a minute, then add the tomato purée. Simmer for a little longer, then add the stock. You will have a lot of liquid but this will gradually evaporate, leaving a very intense flavour. Bring the ragú to simmering point, then let it slowly bubble, barely even boiling, for at least 4 hours. You can also put it in a slow warming oven at 80°C/176°F, overnight. It is ready when the meat is very tender and you have a thick, wet, succulent stew. Add the butter and simmer, then add the pepper. Taste and add salt, only if necessary. Allow to cool.

Make the cheese sauce by heating the milk in a saucepan with the nutmeg and bay leaf. When it reaches boiling point, strain into a jug. Using the same pan, fry the butter and flour together until the mixture is plain and sandy-textured. Slowly whisk in the milk then continue to stir the sauce over the heat until it boils. Add the cheese, cook for a minute, then set to one side.

To assemble:

600g penne

250g cherry tomatoes, halved

1 tsp dried oregano

3 tbsp freshly grated Parmesan cheese

olive oil

Preheat the oven to 190°C/fan 170°C/375°F/Gas 5. Cook the pasta, according to the timing stated on the packet – it should be al dente, with a little firmness in the centre. Drain it and mix into the ragù. Transfer to a large, deep ovenproof dish. Pour over the cheese sauce. Scatter the tomato halves all over the surface. Follow with the oregano and grated Parmesan. Shake over a little olive oil and then bake for about 30 minutes, until the pasta and sauce are bubbling and the top is golden.

Options: Ragù and cheese sauce can be used for lasagna; replace the beef with duck, venison or mixed game, also lamb/mutton.

ROAST SQUASH PUFF PASTRY PIE

with watercress and fresh goat's curd

Serves: 6–8

Serving dish: flat plate or board

1 large butternut squash, quartered and seeds removed

1 tbsp olive oil

500g ready-prepared puff pastry

plain flour, for dusting

salt and freshly ground black pepper

2 bunches watercress, leaves only

250g fresh goat's curd

1 egg, beaten, to glaze

60g butter

½ tsp finely chopped rosemary leaves

½ tsp finely chopped sage leaves

½ tsp thyme leaves

1 garlic clove, peeled

A self-supporting, circular pie, colourful on the inside and packed with good flavours, that short-changes no one. Use the rough puff recipe on page 166 for a meltingly good result; otherwise do buy all-butter puff pastry ready-made.

Preheat the oven to 200°C/fan 180°C/400°F/Gas 6. Rub the squash with the olive oil, place in a roasting tin and bake for about 20 minutes. Remove, allow to cool a little then cut the flesh from the hard skin and slice it. Set to one side.

Cut the pastry in half, dust the worktop with flour and roll out each piece into a circle, slightly larger than the baking sheet. Roll the pastry nice and thin – about 3–4mm thick. Place one piece on the baking sheet.

Arrange the sliced squash directly onto the pastry, leaving a 4cm border around the edge. Work in circles, making the pile slightly higher in the centre. Season with a little salt and pepper as you go. Chop the watercress leaves roughly – do not include any stalks. Put these on top of the squash in an even layer.

Dot the surface with teaspoonfuls of the goat's curd, season with salt and pepper, then brush the edges of the pastry liner with water. Place the second circle of pastry on top and pinch the edges together firmly.

Brush the whole surface with the beaten egg and make a cut in the centre of the pie. Put a ring of pastry around this hole, like a chimney. Score the surface of the pastry very lightly, so as not to pierce it but help it rise. Bake for 35–45 minutes, until golden, then remove from the oven and transfer to a flat plate or board.

Just before serving, melt the butter with the herbs and garlic, letting it bubble. Remove the garlic and, as you serve, pour the flavoured hot butter into the pie chimney. Leave for a couple of minutes for the butter to travel through the filling, then cut large slices and serve.

BROAD BEAN AND PEA TOASTS

Serves: 4

Serving dish: large flat platter or board

400g broad beans
250g petits pois
250g ricotta cheese
20 fresh mint leaves
100g mascarpone
sea salt flakes and freshly ground black pepper
8 slices sourdough bread
6 tbsp extra virgin olive oil, plus extra to serve

A dish for midwinter with broad beans? Yes, because we are using frozen beans, not fresh from the garden. A little patience removing the outer skins from the defrosted broad beans reveals summery green kernels to mash with petits pois and fresh ricotta.

Bring a pan of water to the boil and add the broad beans. Bring back to the boil, then cook for 1 minute and drain. Refresh the beans under the cold tap then pinch the skins to push out the green kernel inside. Place in a bowl and set to one side.

Blanch the petits pois in boiling water for 1 minute then drain and refresh under the cold tap. Shake the colander to remove excess water then put in a food processor with the bean kernels. Blend to a lumpy mash then transfer back to the bowl, adding the ricotta, mint leaves and mascarpone. Season with salt and pepper then mix only partially, so the ingredients are not too well blended. Taste and adjust the seasoning if necessary.

Brush the bread slices on both sides with the olive oil then grill or toast until golden. To serve, heap the bean, pea and cheese mixture onto the toasts, then dribble over a few more drops of extra virgin olive oil.

ROASTED MUSHROOMS ON SOURDOUGH TOAST

with a red wine sauce

Serves: 6–8

Serving dish: individual plates

1kg oyster, king oyster or
  portobello mushrooms,
  or a mix of wild and
  cultivated mushrooms
  (chanterelles/girolles, ceps,
  portobello etc.)
extra virgin olive oil, for
  brushing
salt and freshly ground black
  pepper

For the red wine sauce:

2 large or 8 small shallots,
  finely chopped
2 garlic cloves, chopped
2 tbsp olive oil
2 sprigs thyme
300ml red wine
200ml vegetable stock
120g butter

To serve:

4 slices white sourdough
  bread, brushed with olive
  oil and toasted
2 tbsp chopped flat-leaf
  parsley

Mushrooms on toast, taken to a richer and more festive level using exotic, fleshy king oyster mushrooms and a rich and buttery red wine reduction sauce. This is an ideal dish to serve to everyone for supper. It goes well with a spinach salad, followed by a board with interesting artisan cheeses.

Preheat the oven to 190°C/fan 170°C/375°F/Gas 5. Brush the mushrooms with the olive oil and season with salt and pepper. Place them on a baking sheet and cook until they are golden – about 15 minutes. Remove from the oven and set aside in a warm place. Make the toast and wrap in a cloth to keep it warm without drying out.

To make the sauce, fry the shallots and garlic in the oil, over a medium-low heat, until pale gold. Add the thyme, and then the red wine. Let this bubble for a minute then add the stock – you will have a thin 'gravy'.

Simmer the sauce until it reduces by half, then add the butter and whisk – it will be glossy and thick. Strain it through a sieve and return it to the pan. Spoon the mushrooms over the toast, then pour over the hot sauce. Serve immediately.

CRISPY POTATO CAKES
with garden pea and lettuce sauce

Serves: 6–8

Serving dish: individual plates

Fluffy, light potato cakes in a crisp breadcrumb coating, served with early summer peas – or perfectly delicious frozen petits pois – mint and lettuce.

For the potato cakes:

1.2kg potatoes for mashing, scrubbed, peeled and cut into 2cm dice

4 egg yolks

4 tbsp chopped flat-leaf parsley

sea salt and ground white pepper

4 tbsp plain flour

2 eggs

Pinch of salt

300g fresh breadcrumbs or dry panko breadcrumbs

oil, for frying

For the sauce:

60g butter

2 large shallots, sliced

1 cos or butterhead lettuce, green leaves only

200ml vegetable stock

4 tbsp crème fraîche

400g shelled fresh small garden peas or defrosted frozen petits pois

4 sprigs mint, leaves only, roughly chopped

Bring a pan of water to the boil, add salt and then the potato cubes. Boil for about 6–8 minutes or until just tender – they must not be mushy. Drain the potatoes and let them steam so they become quite dry. Put them in a bowl and mash them or pass them through a vegetable mill (mouli-legumes). Add the egg yolks and parsley to the bowl, mix well then season with salt and pepper. Chill to firm up the mixture.

Form the potato mix into cakes, about 5cm in diameter and 2cm thick. Have ready three shallow bowls: put the flour in one, the eggs in the second and beat them with a little salt, then put the breadcrumbs in the third.

Dip each cake in the flour, coating it all over, then coat it in the egg, then finally breadcrumbs. Set the cakes to one side while you make the sauce.

Melt the butter in a pan, then add the shallots and sauté over a low-medium heat until soft. Add the lettuce leaves with the stock. Simmer for 1–2 minutes until the lettuce is soft, then put in a food processor or liquidiser with 2 tablespoons of the crème fraîche and blend until you have a smooth, thin sauce.

Fry the potato cakes in the oil, then put a couple on each plate – or more. Blanch the peas in boiling water for 1 minute. Add to the sauce with the mint leaves, season to taste and then spoon around the potato cakes. Eat straight away.

SIDES

In recent times, side dishes have evolved into a far more interesting palette. Where once some boiled seasonal greens and a few potato options would do for any dinner, now I think that we can expect more – if only on occasion. I still think a bubbling dish of good potato dauphinoise is exactly what many meat-based main courses need for companionship, but then why not tap into the availability of multi-coloured 'heritage' carrots and make an unusually pretty salad? Often these choices come down to having enough time for preparation. Having said that, a few green leaves dressed with olive oil are a perfectly adequate side vegetable when you are in a hurry.

When possible, serve seasonal vegetables as sides. There is a sensibility about this; it feels and looks right and during the glut season for each vegetable they are at their best – not least good value for money. I do not want to make a hard and fast rule, however. Seasons for certain vegetables grown in Britain have become extended and even perpetual due to modern growing and storage methods. Tomatoes, for example, are now grown all year round using environmentally economical technology and some new breeds taste surprisingly sweet even for winter. And anyway, sometimes it is nice to taste summer, mid-February.

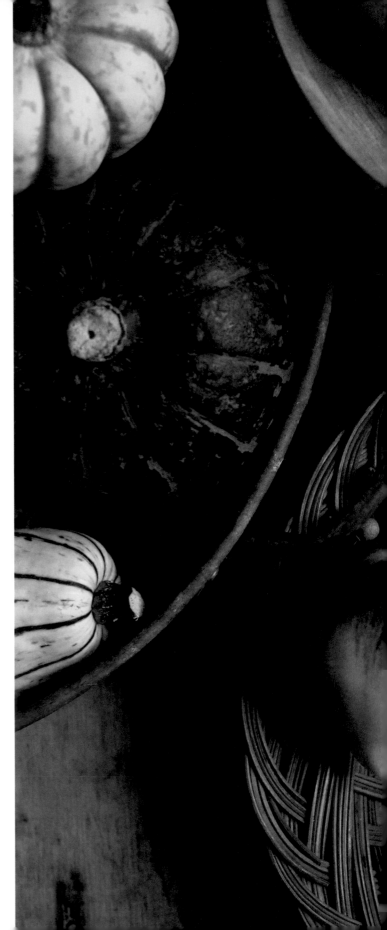

For larger, help-yourself-to-food parties, increasing the number of side dishes offered is helpful because it stretches the main meat or fish dish. I find that people love to try everything while not piling their plates too high, so they will not take huge amounts of fish pie, for example, when there are four interesting vegetables to try. On these occasions, extra vegetable side dishes will also satisfy vegetarian guests.

TOMATO SALADS

Serves 6–8

Serving dish: large bowl

1 kg mixed tomatoes: baby plum or cherries, yellow, striped 'tiger' tomatoes, large plums and beef tomatoes – whatever is available.

1 handful basil leaves

6 tbsp extra virgin olive oil

Ingredients of your choice (see method)

salt and fresh ground black pepper, to taste

It's about the tomatoes. We have a huge variety to choose from now, including many traditional shapes and colours, the so-called 'heritage' breeds. Cut and slice, leave them whole, dress with extra virgin olive oil and basil. You can also pair them with many ingredients – see below.

For a classic, peeled tomato salad use ripe plum tomatoes. Nick each one with a knife. Boil a kettle and pour the water into a bowl and add the tomatoes. Leave for 1-1 ½ minutes, then drain. Peel the tomatoes. Cut lengthways and remove the seeds. Cut into strips then dress with extra virgin olive oil.

Other variations include:

Tomato with mint and black olives

Tomato with mint, cucumber, barrel-aged feta cheese, sliced shallot and black olives

Tomato, buffalo mozzarella and basil

Tomato with shaved fennel and green olives

Tomato with white haricot beans, garlic and basil

Tomato with fine green beans and shallot (optional)

Tomato and artichoke

Dress all with extra virgin olive oil.

FAIL-SAFE ROAST POTATOES

Serves: 6–8

*Serving dish: a
warmed bowl*

8–12 medium-large Maris
  Piper or other good
  roasting potatoes
2 sprigs each rosemary,
  thyme and sage (optional)
extra virgin olive oil

*I always teach people to cook potatoes this way now. It makes very crispy roast
potatoes and they stay crispy, too. It never fails if you use extra virgin olive oil and
stick with the recommended cooking temperature. Do not use a higher temperature
or you will spoil the oil. Excess oil can be sieved through kitchen paper and reused in
cooking, though not for salads.*

Preheat the oven to 190°C/fan 170°C/375°F/Gas 5. Peel the potatoes then
cut into quarters. I tend to make long-shaped quarters because they look
attractive – but there is no rule. Put them in a large pan and cover with cold
water. Bring to the boil and par-cook for 7 minutes. The potatoes should be
beginning to break up on the outside and irm in the middle.

Put the potatoes and the herbs (if using) in a roasting pan and toss them in
enough oil to make sure they are well covered. Put them in the oven and roast
for 50–60 minutes, or until golden and crisp. Transfer to a warmed dish and
serve or keep warm until needed.

BAKED SLICED POTATOES
with stock and garlic

Serves: 6–8

Serving dish: 25cm round roasting tin

4 tbsp soft butter

8–10 medium King Edward, Maris Piper or other maincrop potatoes, washed and peeled

4 garlic cloves, thinly sliced

sea salt and freshly ground black pepper

400ml chicken or vegetable stock (see page 62)

This is my version of potatoes bonne femme, a sort of dauphinoise (creamy baked sliced potatoes) but without the cream. You can vary the amount of garlic depending on what goes with it, but either way it is an utterly good potato dish, which keeps warm nicely after cooking and can even be made the day before, covered with foil once cooled then reheated. Don't overcook the potatoes – once you can insert a fork, they are done. For a rich version, replace half the stock with double cream. Also, you can make a rustic version without peeling the potatoes – just make sure to wash them very well.

Preheat the oven to 190°C/fan 170°C/375°F/Gas 5. Rub the inside of the roasting tin with half the butter. Slice the potatoes very thinly (1–2mm) on a mandolin, or use the slicing tool on a food processor. You can, if you have a sharp knife, slice the potatoes by hand quite easily.

Scatter a layer of potatoes on the base of the tin. Add a couple of pieces of garlic, a grind of black pepper, a pinch of salt and then another layer of potato. Continue until the roasting tin is full, even piled up (the potatoes collapse down during cooking).

Pour in the stock – just enough so that ⅓ of the potatoes are not submerged. Dot the remaining butter over the surface and bake for 35–40 minutes or until the potatoes can be easily pierced with a fork. Serve or keep warm.

POMMES PURÉE

Serves: 6–8

Serving dish: a warmed bowl

12–16 medium-sized King
 Edward, Maris Piper or
 other maincrop potatoes,
 washed and peeled
600ml whole milk
200g butter
sea salt and ground white
 pepper

Potatoes, not mashed but transformed to a smooth purée, lightened with scalded milk but also enriched with butter. I was taught to make pommes purée at my grandmother's house in France and, much as I love stalwart, stand-up-by-itself British mash, I was won over by the rippling pool of potato served with Toulouse sausages or smoked frankfurters. The scalded milk in the recipe is important; it gives the potatoes a slight tang. I use a hand-held mouli-lEgumes or food mill, but the same effect can be achieved with a potato ricer or grater. The grater on a food processor can also be used.

Cut the potatoes into quarters, put them in a pan of salted cold water and bring to the boil. Boil them for 10 minutes, until soft in the centre, then tip into a colander. Let them sit steaming in the colander for about 15 minutes, to dry out. Some people put the colander (if metal) into a warming oven (70°C/158°F) to help the process.

Put the milk and butter in the empty potato pan. Bring to simmering point; let the butter melt without the milk boiling, so keep the heat low. Remove from the heat. Place a food mill (mouli-legumes) or potato ricer over the pan and pass the potatoes through it. You can also grate the potato through a medium grater.

Place the pan over a low heat and slowly beat and stir the potatoes over it, so they do not stick to the base, until the purée is steaming hot and bubbles somewhat volcanically and slowly. Season with salt and white pepper, to taste. Keep the potato moving as you take it off the heat and cover with a cloth to keep warm until needed.

KALE WITH APPLE AND WALNUTS

Serves: 6–8

Serving dish: *salad bowl*

200g walnut halves

2 tbsp vegetable oil

700g kale

4 eating apples, cored and
  sliced thinly

8 tbsp extra virgin olive oil

sea salt and freshly ground
  black pepper

I have enthusiastically joined the legion of kale fans, but only now I know it must be properly cooked, cooled and dried before dressing it. The apples and walnuts go gorgeously; this is a salad on its own but also very good alongside roast gammon or pork. Choose kale that feels tactile and looks green. Very woody stalks indicate tough leaves.

Toast the walnuts in a pan with the vegetable oil over a very low heat for about 10 minutes, shaking the pan from time to time to turn them. Tip onto a sheet of kitchen towel and set to one side.

Wash the kale and cut out any tough stalks. Chop it into 1–2cm shreds. Bring a large pan of water to the boil and add the kale. Boil it for 1–5 minutes – how quickly it becomes tender to the bite will vary, but do not overcook it; it is better to err on the side of underdone.

When cooked, remove the pan from the heat and drain the kale in a colander. Refresh with plenty of very cold water to fix the colour. Next, take handfuls and squeeze out all excess water. The kale, if not overcooked, should bounce back nicely. Put it in a salad bowl. Add the apples and walnuts and then dress with the oil and season with sea salt and black pepper.

GREENS

with lemon and rosemary butter

Serves: 6–8

Serving dish: a warmed bowl

1.5kg greens, washed, the hard stalks and tough leaves removed: choose two types or more (e.g. green cabbage, savoy cabbage, spring greens, Hispi (pointed cabbage), kale, romanesco, purple sprouting broccoli, sprout tops, cavolo nero)

2 tsp salt

For the lemon and rosemary butter:

½ tsp sea salt

½ tsp freshly ground black pepper

150g butter

2 sprigs rosemary, leaves only

zest of 1 lemon

This seems rather obvious but the purpose of giving a recipe for cooking greens is to talk more about the leafy brassicas, that is the cabbage family, themselves. I know that a lot of people shudder to see cabbage – a result of school dinners and bad memories probably. These vegetables are beautiful to look at but are often packed severely trimmed, in plastic bags – not very appetising. I admit I do share a gloomy view of overcooked greens, and they can taste a little sulphurous, but this can be rectified by keeping cooking times short, removing hard stalks and dressing them with the magic combination of rosemary and lemon. I do not add the juice of the lemon because it turns everything grey, but you can do this at the last minute.

Bring a large pan of water to the boil. Prepare the greens by cutting the leaves if they are too large. Add the salt to the water and then the larger, tougher leaves like sprout tops and savoy cabbage. Cook for 2 minutes then add the tender greens like spring cabbage, romanesco and purple sprouting. Simmer for another 3–5 minutes, checking that the leaves are just tender. Drain in a colander and refresh with cold water, shaking the colander to make sure the cold water reaches all the leaves. Leave to stand and drain then tip onto a clean tea towel to make sure that all the water has run away.

Meanwhile, for the lemon and rosemary butter put all the ingredients except the lemon zest in a small pan and bring to the boil. Simmer for a minute then add to the big pan with the greens, toss in the heat until they are warmed through, then scatter with the lemon zest. Toss once more and serve.

FLAGEOLET BEANS
and cavolo nero purée

Serves: 6–8

Serving dish: large bowl

6 plum or large ripe
   tomatoes
80g unsalted butter
2 large or 6 small shallots,
   finely chopped
175ml white wine
900g canned flageolet beans,
   drained

For the purée:
60g butter
250g cavolo nero, leaves
   only, chopped
400ml vegetable stock
salt and freshly ground black
   pepper

A favourite winter stew, and a recipe from one of my neighbours. The cavolo nero is a stunning green when puréed, quite a surprise. Serve with Parmesan croutons (see page 63) or over pasta for a filling dish.

First make the purée. Melt the butter and add the chopped cavolo leaves. Add the stock and simmer for 10 minutes, or until the leaves are very tender. Transfer to a food processor and blend until you have a smooth purée. Add a little salt and pepper to taste.

Nick the skins of the plum tomatoes with a sharp knife, then put them in a deep bowl. Pour over boiling water and leave for 2 minutes. Drain and then skin the tomatoes, quarter them and remove the seeds. Chop them into 1cm dice and set to one side.

Melt the butter in a large pan and add the shallots. Cook over a medium-low heat until the shallots are soft then add the wine. Allow to bubble for a few minutes then add the beans and the tomatoes. Once the dish is simmering again, stir in the purée. Taste and adjust the seasoning, and serve.

Options: Use white haricot or cannellini beans instead of flageolet.

BRAISED LENTILS

Serves: 6–8

Serving dish: casserole or saucepan

4 tbsp olive oil

2 onions, finely chopped

1 large carrot, finely diced

2 celery sticks, finely diced

3 garlic cloves, finely chopped

2 tsp dried thyme

1 bay leaf

350g Puy lentils

2 tbsp tomato purée

150ml red wine

750ml vegetable stock or water

4 tbsp extra virgin olive oil

sea salt and freshly ground black pepper

chopped flat-leaf parsley, to serve

Use Puy or similar small green-grey marbled lentils to make this natural braise. I often make a casserole of these to serve as a side dish to potatoes, especially if I am worried I have not bought a large enough joint of meat.

Heat the oil and add the vegetables, garlic and herbs. Fry over a medium-low heat until soft, then add the lentils. Fry for a minute then add the tomato purée. Cook for a further minute, then add the wine and let it bubble for about 30 seconds.

Add the stock or water and bring to simmering point. Simmer the lentils for about 25 minutes – the only way to tell if they are done is to bite or cut one. They should be only just tender in the centre – al dente but without any rawness. Remove from the heat and immediately tip into a bowl to cool them and prevent further cooking. Stir in the extra virgin olive oil, season to taste with salt and pepper, then serve with a sprinkling of chopped parsley.

The lentils keep well in a warm place and are also delicious served cold.

MACARONI CHEESE

Serves: 6–8

Serving dish: shallow (4–7cm deep) ovenproof dish

1.5 litres whole milk

a few gratings of nutmeg

1 bay leaf

2 tbsp plain flour

2 tbsp butter

100g grated Cheddar cheese

100g grated Emmental cheese, plus extra to sprinkle over the top

30g grated Parmesan cheese, plus extra to sprinkle over the top

salt and freshly ground black pepper

3 tbsp double cream

500g dried macaroni or cavatappi (twisted tubes, very successful for macaroni)

The revival of mac 'n' cheese as a side is ongoing. I am ambivalent about whether it should be served alongside steak or pulled pork, because I am happy to eat it alone. But it is another recipe that, if on the table, ensures that there is something for everyone. And children love it, too. Make sure to cook the macaroni fully or they absorb the sauce when baking, drying out the dish.

Preheat the oven to 190°C/fan 170°C/375°F/Gas 5 – if possible set it to use the fan oven with grill. Bring a very large pan of water – about 5 litres – to the boil.

Heat the milk to boiling point with the nutmeg and bay leaf. Remove from the heat and set to one side. Put the flour and butter in a large saucepan and fry until sandy and pale. Add the milk, whisking, then keep stirring to avoid lumps forming while the sauce comes back to the boil, thickening. Add the cheeses and, once they have melted, season to taste. Add the cream and remove from the heat.

Meanwhile, cook the pasta in the boiling water, timing it according to the packet instructions. When it is cooked through, drain it and shake off any excess water. Put the pasta in a shallow ovenproof dish. Pour over the cheese sauce, letting it work its way down to the bottom, perhaps helping it with a spoon but not stirring.

Scatter extra cheese all over the top. Bake the macaroni for about 15–20 minutes until bubbling and golden. Ideally, eat it straight away but it will keep warm.

PUDDINGS
& BAKING

The child in us all wishes every dinner or party to end sweetly. These sweet endings can be effortless: a bowl of fruit; a box of dates or chocolates; a bought-in tart or tub of ice cream; or quite often a kind friend might bring a pudding – a saviour if desserts are not your favourite course to cook. I make no judgement on whether every dinner ends in pudding. I find not everyone has a sweet tooth, and a proportion of people always turn it down. Often, I serve cheese instead and then some chocolates with tea or coffee. If I know a guest loves their puddings, I will make one regardless; ergo, I usually make puddings if there are children coming, especially for lunch on Sunday.

If you are new to preparing three-course dinners, avoid making those that need to be cooked at the same time as the main course or starter. I have burned many a crumble top using the same oven space as roast potatoes, and have since learned to make crumble that keeps warm without going soggy (see page 138). There are also some winning puddings that must be made the day before, like crème caramel, chocolate mousse and ice cream, and these are the ones I recommend for novice dinner hosts because they get the pudding course well out of the way.

Stating the obvious, successful puddings come with good recipes. You want well-behaved meringues, pastry that will not shrink and sponges that rise, not sink. The recipes that follow are such a collection and there is something here, I think, to please everyone.

I am a keen baker and if time allows I regard it as a pleasure not a chore. Making a pretty if slightly lopsided, jam-stuffed Victoria sponge and decorating it with strawberries for a friend's celebration is an act of love. Giving guests warm bread or rolls almost straight from the oven is a kindness. I think baking is very much a task to undertake for your own pleasure – and that is fine, just as it is to throw money at the situation and buy good bread or cakes.

I used to run a small artisan bakery and became fascinated by the science and sensory side of baking. It was all about finding the best recipes. Mastering brioche was so exciting and yet such a relief because it was not that difficult.

You can buy flatbreads of all sorts, especially if you are lucky enough to live near Asian and Middle Eastern shops. Yet making your own is easy and, if you live miles away from a good source, the know-how is handy. In the West Country, I regularly make flatbreads when preparing Indian dishes. The dough can be made the day before and actually benefits from being left overnight for a slow 'prove' in the fridge. One hour before dinner it needs to be shaped into balls, then 30 minutes later stretched flat and baked.

Simple sponges, dusted with sugar and artfully dotted with fruit, will never equal professionally iced cakes but they possess unapologetic homemade charm.

Mixers, baking equipment and suppliers of specialist ingredients can be found in the Directory on pages 268–72.

CHOCOLATE MOUSSE

Serves: 6–8

Serving dish: 6–8 x 100ml ramekins (tea or coffee cups will also do)

400g dark chocolate (minimum 70% cocoa solids)

3 tbsp strong coffee (preferably espresso)

60g unsalted butter

6 eggs, separated

pinch of cream of tartar

2 tsp caster sugar

One of the greats to emerge from seventies bistro cooking culture, derived from the French pot au chocolat, chocolate mousse is an intense and rich chocolate manifestation. For chocolate buffs, the eggs enhance good chocolate, which I urge you to buy when making this pudding.

Break up the chocolate and put it in a ceramic bowl with the coffee and butter. Set this over a small saucepan of barely boiling water and melt the chocolate, stirring occasionally.

Beat the egg yolks into the chocolate mixture while it is still over the hot water. Remove from the heat and allow to cool a little so it is still creamy enough to stir easily.

Put the egg whites in a bowl and whisk until foamy. Add the cream of tartar then whisk until you have soft white peaks. Add the caster sugar and whisk until glossy and firm.

Fold 2 tablespoons of the egg white into the chocolate mixture, stirring well to loosen the texture. Scrape the chocolate mixture into the egg white bowl, then fold both together well – there must not be any pockets of white egg foam. You should have a dark cream with bubbles.

Transfer to the ramekins then put in the fridge and chill until set. The chocolate mousses will keep well, covered with clingfilm, for about 3 days.

HAZELNUT AND RASPBERRY MERINGUE

Serves: 6–8

Serving dish: flat plate

100g shelled, skinned
 hazelnuts
4 egg whites
270g icing sugar, sifted
200ml double cream,
 whipped
400g raspberries

The partnership of toasted hazels and raspberries is a classic for summer parties. Do buy hazelnuts that have already been skinned – skinning them after toasting is messy work. You will need an electric tabletop mixer or a powerful electric hand whisk. Can be made up to 3 hours before serving.

Preheat the oven to 180°C/fan 160°C/350°F/Gas 4. Put the skinned hazelnuts on a baking sheet and toast in the oven until golden. Remove from the oven and allow to cool, then grind to a powder in a food processor. Turn the oven down to 150°C/fan 130°C/300°F/Gas 2.

Put the egg whites and icing sugar in the bowl of an electric mixer and whisk for 8–10 minutes until you have a stiff meringue. Fold in the ground hazelnuts.

Line two baking sheets with baking parchment and then spoon an equal amount of meringue into the centre of each. Spread each into a 20cm disc. Bake for 35–40 minutes until the meringue is crisp and beginning to rise, with bubbles around the base. Remove from the oven and allow to cool.

Turn one of the meringue discs over – hazelnut meringue can be quite fragile but don't be too put off if it breaks. Place it on a flat plate and peel off the parchment paper. Spread the cream onto it then scatter over the raspberries. Turn over the second meringue disc, and peel off the baking parchment. Turn it the right way up and lay it on top of the first, then serve.

APPLE CRUMBLE

Serves: 6–8

*Serving dish: 30 x 20cm
ovenproof dish*

about 1kg dessert apples,
    peeled, cored and cut into
    1cm dice
golden caster sugar, to
    sweeten if necessary
½ tsp ground cinnamon

For the crumble:
100g plain flour
50g ground almonds
125g chilled, unsalted butter,
    cubed
35g demerara sugar
35g golden caster sugar
2 tbsp water

*For many years crumbles were my nemesis. The crumble mix would somehow
always become submerged in the juices of the fruit, creating horrible wet clods
of ballast underneath. It was, in the end, a newspaper article that came to the
rescue, suggesting adding a few drops of water to the mix to bring parts of it
together. It works.*

Preheat the oven to 200°C/fan 180°C/400°F/Gas 6.

Heap the apples into the ovenproof dish, and, if they are sour, add 1–2
dessertspoons of sugar. It is nice for the apple part to be quite tart, however.
Add the cinnamon and mix well.

Put the flour, ground almonds and butter into a bowl and rub the butter into
the flour with your fingertips – to breadcrumb consistency. Stir in the sugars.
If you have a food processor I recommend putting all the crumble ingredients
except the water into it and giving it a quick blitz – to get the same effect
without the butter softening.

With the crumble in a bowl, drip a little of the water onto the surface and rake
through with a fork to form lumps. Add a little more until you have a lumpy
but loose mixture. Do not add more than 2 tablespoonfuls or you will end up
with pastry.

Spoon the crumble onto the apples, then bake for 30–40 minutes until the
crumble top is golden and the apples bubbling around it. Remove from the
oven and allow to cool a little, to stop further cooking, then store in a warm
place before serving. Crumble reheats well.

TARTE AUX POMMES

Serves: 6–8

Serving dish: flat board

6–8 eating apples
plain flour, for dusting
300g ready-made all-butter
   puff pastry
4 tbsp apricot jam
juice of ½ lemon
1 tbsp water

You would never know, looking at the neat mosaic of thinly sliced apple laid onto the thinnest of golden pastry crusts, that a French apple tart is a handy emergency pudding. With apples, some frozen ready-made puff pastry and a pot of apricot jam, you can be your own patisserie. You can of course also make this tart using the pastry recipe on page 166. It will not add much more than 45 minutes to the cooking time.

Preheat the oven to 200°C/fan 180°C/400°F/Gas 6 and line a baking sheet with baking parchment.

Cut around the core of the apples, but do not peel them. Slice the apples thinly into semi-circles.

Dust the worktop with flour and roll out the pastry until very thin, no more than 2mm thick, then trim into a 30 x 20cm rectangle. Pick the sheet of pastry up by rolling it onto the rolling pin and unrolling it onto the baking sheet.

Prick the pastry all over with a fork, except for a 1cm border. Arrange the apple slices on the pastry in neat rows, overlapping each other, within the border.

Bake the tart for 15–25 minutes until the pastry is golden and also crisp underneath. The apples should be soft and browned in places.

Remove the tart from the oven and allow it to cool. Put the apricot jam in a saucepan with the lemon juice and water and bring to the boil. Simmer for a few minutes then pass the jam through a sieve. Use the sieved jam to glaze the tart, painting it on with a pastry brush. Allow to set then cut the tart into pieces and serve.

CARAMELISED ORANGES
with salt

Serves: 6–8

Serving dish: shallow dish that is mildly heat resistant, i.e. dishwasher-proof.

6–8 best-quality oranges
200g caster sugar
½ tsp salt

In retro mindset with a pudding that was all the rage at dinner parties and with a reason – because it is a winner. It looks wonderful, and the flavour of the smoky sugar with the oranges is a classic. I have dragged the recipe into the twenty-first century with the addition of salt which does benefit the taste, knocking the edge off the sweetness of the original. Try it with blood oranges when they come into season, also with tangerines or satsumas. Make this just before your guests arrive – the caramel should stay crisp for about 1½ hours.

Using a very sharp knife, pare the skin from the oranges completely so the edges are raw. Then slice them across the segments, no more than 1cm thick. Arrange them on a dish. Put the sugar in a saucepan and add enough water to just soak it. Add the salt and very slowly heat it, so that all the sugar dissolves. Do not stir it but agitate the pan slightly. Use a pastry brush dipped in water to keep the sides of the pan clean. This is to prevent crystallisation.

Boil the caramel until it begins to colour and become deliciously fragrant, then watch it until it is chestnut brown, not dark or smoking. As soon as you judge it ready, pour it all over the oranges, keeping the pan moving all the time. It will bubble and set. It can be served as soon as you like.

Clean the pan by filling it with water and bringing to boiling point.

CRÈME CARAMEL

Serves: 6–8

*Serving dish: 6–8 x 100ml
ramekins*

200g caster sugar

For the crème:
750ml milk
½ vanilla pod, seeds only
2 tsp sugar
3 eggs plus 3 egg yolks

To serve:
double cream
fresh soft fruits or compote

A classic pudding and among my favourites, not least because you can make crème caramel three days in advance of dinner. Almost everyone adores it. The secret is to slightly undercook, so the texture is sublimely silky. It is a matter of reading the wobble . . .

Preheat the oven to 150°C/fan 130°C/300°F/Gas 2.

Put the sugar in a heavy-based pan and add enough water to soak it. Place over a very low heat until the sugar melts. Do not stir or the caramel will crystallise. Swirl in the pan to help dissolve the sugar. Use a wet pastry brush to keep the sides of the pan clean after swirling the pan.

When the sugar has mostly dissolved, bring slowly to the boil. Boil over a medium heat until the caramel turns golden brown and smells deliciously fragrant – do not wait until it is dark. Have the ramekins to hand. Pour a little caramel straight from the pan into a ramekin, then tilt to cover the base and sides. Repeat with the other ramekins. Work as quickly as you can and be careful not to burn yourself. The caramel will set immediately. You can clean the pan by filling it with water and boiling it.

To make the crème, heat the milk in a saucepan with the vanilla and sugar. Put the eggs and egg yolks in a bowl and whisk in the milk mixture. Pass through a sieve into a jug then fill each ramekin.

Boil the kettle. Place the ramekins in a roasting pan and add about 1–2cm of hot water to the pan, being careful not to splash any into the ramekins. Bake for 25 minutes or until the crème sets, but still wobbles. Remove from the oven. Lift out the ramekins and set them in a dish with cold water to cool them quickly. Place in the fridge for at least 2 hours, or overnight.

To turn out, run a knife around the edge of each ramekin and invert the crème caramels onto individual plates. Serve with a little double cream and some fresh fruit or compote.

BERRY TRIFLE

Serves: 6–8

Serving dish: 2.5-litre deep glass bowl

200g sponge fingers
200g berry jam
100ml kirsch
100ml pure pressed apple juice
1kg fresh berries
1 litre good-quality fresh vanilla custard
1 litre double cream
1 tbsp toasted flaked almonds

Layers of sponge fingers, jam, custard, berries, whipped cream and more fresh berries, a bountiful trifle will always be the overdressed diva of the pudding table. A bit old fashioned but no one minds as they devour the ticklish textures – a good trifle brings pure joy. The availability of good-quality fresh custard provides a welcome shortcut – trifles used to take twice as long to make. Use any seasonal berry, and a corresponding jam.

Spread the sponge fingers with jam and layer them in the base of the bowl. Pour over the kirsch and apple juice as you layer the fingers. Add about half the fruit, then pour over the custard.

Whip the cream until it is soft and thick. Spoon it over the custard, then scatter over the remaining fruit and the flaked almonds.

ICED CHOCOLATE PARFAIT

Serves: 6–8

*Serving dish: 1-litre loaf tin
(20 x 8 x 10cm), or similar
plastic container*

225g dark chocolate
(minimum 70% cocoa
solids)

2 tbsp strong coffee
(espresso is ideal)

30g butter

6 eggs, separated

80g caster sugar

1.5 tbsp clear honey

5 sheets leaf gelatine

110ml double cream

½tsp cream of tartar

*In many ways this is another type of mousse, served frozen. I have included gelatine
because the parfait melts quickly after being removed from the tin and the gelatine
holds it in place. It also adds unctuousness to the pudding. It is fun to serve with
'cigarettes russes', those old-fashioned rolled-up wafers dipped in chocolate.*

Line the loaf tin with two pieces of baking parchment, measuring 19 x 30cm and
8 x 30 cm. Insert them into the mould, one lengthways, one across.

Break up the chocolate and put it in a ceramic bowl with the coffee and butter.
Set over a small saucepan of simmering water until the chocolate has melted,
stirring occasionally. Remove from the heat, then beat in the egg yolks while it
is still warm. Stir in 60g of the caster sugar and the honey and set to one side.

Put the gelatine sheets in a bowl and cover with cold water. Soak for a few
minutes and then use your hands to squeeze out all the water from the soft
gelatine sheets.

Put the cream in a pan and heat to just above hand hot (do not let it boil).
Add the gelatine sheets and stir until they are completely dissolved, keeping
the temperature low so that they set the pudding well. Stir the cream into the
chocolate mixture.

Put the egg whites in a bowl and whisk until foamy. Add the cream of tartar,
then whisk until you have soft white peaks. Add the rest of the caster sugar
and whisk until glossy and firm. Scrape the chocolate mixture into the egg
white bowl, then fold both together well – there must not be any pockets of
white egg foam. Pour the mixture into the tin, right up to the top.

Place it in the freezer. It will be fully frozen within 2 hours. To unmould,
remove from the freezer 5 minutes before serving. Place a flat plate on top
of it and turn the tin upside down, then remove the paper. Serve in slices.

CHOU CHOU PUDDING

Serves: 6–8

Serving dish: flat plate

90g shelled unsalted peanuts

4 egg whites

270g icing sugar, sifted

150ml double cream, whipped

2–3 bananas, peeled and sliced

100g shop-bought dulce de leche or caramel sauce

juice of 1 lime

For the sugared peanuts:

2 tbsp demerara sugar

3 tbsp shelled unsalted peanuts

A joint venture between an old memory and my daughter Lara, who suggested my list of puddings needed one from the school of 'never sticky enough'. The result is deliberately sweet on sweet, with a peanut macaroon sandwich; cream, caramel and bananas inside. On top is my contribution – sugared peanuts, or 'chou chou' as the French call them, and as I first knew them on family holidays. You will need an electric tabletop mixer or a powerful electric hand whisk.

Preheat the oven to 180°C/fan 160°C/350°F/Gas 4. Put the peanuts on a baking sheet and toast in the oven until golden and fragrant, about 8 minutes. Watch that they do not overcook. Remove them and then grind to a powder in a food processor. Turn the oven down to 150°C/fan 130°C/300°F/Gas 2.

Put the egg whites and icing sugar in the bowl of an electric mixer and whisk for 8–10 minutes until you have a stiff meringue. Fold in the ground peanuts. Line two baking sheets with baking parchment and then spoon an equal amount of meringue into the centre of each. Spread each into a 20cm disc. Bake for 35–40 minutes until the meringue is crisp and beginning to rise, with bubbles around the base. Remove from the oven and allow to cool.

Meanwhile, prepare the sugared peanuts. Put the demerara sugar in a small saucepan and melt it over a medium heat. Let it bubble for 2 minutes then add the peanuts. Cook them in the sugar until it crystallises and begins to break up. Tip the sugared peanuts onto a heatproof surface and use a table knife to separate them if they are stuck together. Allow them to cool.

Turn one of the peanut meringue discs over – it will be quite firm. Place it on a flat plate and peel off the parchment paper. Spread the cream on top of it. Dress the bananas with the lime juice then scatter over the cream and spoon over the caramel sauce. Turn over the second meringue disc, and peel off the baking parchment. Turn it the right way up and lay it on top of the first. Scatter over the sugared peanuts and serve.

PINK GRAPEFRUIT SORBET

Serves: 6–8

*Serving dish: individual
glasses or coupes*

2 egg whites
150g icing sugar
600ml freshly squeezed pink
grapefruit juice

Fresh fruit water ices and sorbets are very easy to make at home, with or without an ice-cream churner. They are ideal after very rich first and second courses, and on hot summer nights. Try the same recipe with lemon, orange or blood orange (my favourite in midwinter).

Whisk together the egg whites with the icing sugar until you have a smooth, bubbly cream. Combine this with the grapefruit juice. If you have an ice-cream machine, process the sorbet following the maker's instructions, churning it until pale pink, opaque and stiff. Put the churn container in the deep freeze to store. Alternatively, without an ice-cream maker, transfer the mixture into a container and place in the deep freeze. After 30 minutes stir, then freeze again. Repeat 3–4 times, then store the container in the freezer. Remove from the deep freeze 10 minutes or so before serving. To serve, scoop from the frozen container into glasses or coupes.

LIMONCELLO CRÊPES

Serves: 6–8

*Serving dish: medium-large
shallow ovenproof dish*

175g fine plain white flour

2 large eggs

60g unsalted butter, melted
and cooled, plus extra for
frying

500ml creamy whole milk

1 tbsp lemon zest ribbons,
made with a zester

crème fraîche, to serve

For the lemon cream:

150g softened unsalted
butter

150g icing sugar

zest of 2 lemons

juice of 1 lemon

70ml Limoncello or juice
of 1 extra lemon (if
you don't want a boozy
pudding)

*Crêpes Suzette, overhauled with a lemon tipple. These pancakes are exceptionally
rich and good; a useful recipe not just for puddings but also for making simple
pancakes with lemon or syrup on Shrove Tuesday, for breakfast or other feasts.*

Preheat the oven to 200°C/fan 180°C/400°F/Gas 6. Sieve the flour into a bowl
and add the eggs and butter – stir well. Bit by bit beat in the milk until you
have a smooth, creamy batter. Leave to stand for 30 minutes before frying.

Place a large non-stick frying pan (20–25cm) over a medium-high heat, add
a small knob of butter and brush it all over the surface of the pan – I find a
silicone pastry 'brush' ideal for this.

Pour 50ml – about half a regular soup ladle – of batter into the pan and tilt in
a circular motion to spread over the base. Aim to make very thin pancakes.
Cook until the edges and underside are golden brown, then flip over with a
palette knife. Cook for another 30 seconds or so, being careful not to burn
the underside. It should have pale brown spots. Remember that the first will
never be a great pancake. Tip the pancake out onto a plate.

Make the rest, using a little more butter each time or if the pan seems dry,
swirling a small knob around until it melts and foams. Keep all the pancakes
warm in a pile, a clean tea towel over them.

Beat together the lemon cream ingredients. Place a spoonful of the lemon
cream inside each pancake, then fold in 4, like a cornet, . Put them in the
ovenproof dish, overlapping each other in two rows. Scatter over the lemon
zest ribbons. If you have any extra lemon cream, drizzle a little over the
arranged pancakes.

Bake for 15–20 minutes until the edges of the pancakes are crisp and all is
bubbling. Serve hot, with a spoonful of crème fraîche.

RASPBERRY ANGEL FOOD CAKE
with raspberry jam and cream

Serves: 6–8

Serving dish: cake stand or flat plate; you will need a 20cm non-stick angel food cake tin (see Directory, page 271)

30g butter, for greasing
180g plain white flour (use finely milled cake flour)
30g cornflour
350g caster sugar, plus extra for dusting
12 egg whites
1 tsp cream of tartar
1 tsp vanilla essence
500g fresh raspberries

To serve
good-quality raspberry jam
whipped cream

A cake-meringue hybrid, which must be made in a ring cake mould to rise evenly. The airy, sticky texture of angel food cake contrasts impeccably with fresh and juicy raspberries, jam and cream.

Preheat the oven to 160°C/fan 140°C/325°F/Gas 3. To prepare the tin, grease generously with the butter, then dust with a layer of caster sugar.

Sieve the flour with the cornflour and add 275g of the caster sugar. Whisk to combine. Put the egg whites in a large bowl with the cream of tartar and use an electric whisk to beat to a stiff foam. Add the remaining sugar and whisk again until glossy.

Stir in the vanilla essence, then sieve the flour mixture into the egg white. Fold in lightly and swiftly, then transfer the mixture to the cake tin. Tap the tin a couple of times on the worktop, then smooth the surface absolutely level with a spatula.

Bake until the cake shrinks away from the edges – about 45–55 minutes. It will be golden on the surface. Cool in the tin for 10 minutes then turn out and continue to cool on a rack.

Arrange the raspberries on the surface, in rows or randomly, whichever suits you. Serve the cake at the table, cutting big slices, and pass around the raspberry jam and cream.

COCOA-ALMOND CAKE

Serves: 8–10

Equipment: *25cm cake tin with loose base*

Serving dish: *plate or board*

225g butter, softened, plus extra for greasing the tin

plain or rice flour, for dusting the tin

50g cocoa powder, plus extra for dusting (optional)

100ml boiling water

1 tsp vanilla extract

225g caster sugar

6 medium eggs, separated

170g ground almonds

pinch of salt

¾ tsp cream of tartar

icing sugar, for dusting (optional)

For the ganache glaze (optional):

120g double cream

120g grated unsweetened dark chocolate (minimum 70% cocoa solids)

To decorate (optional):

deep red, edible rose petals

little pieces edible gold leaf

Flourless and slightly sunken in the centre, this is soggy while being light at the same time. It makes a lovely celebration cake to serve at dinner, with whipped cream. You do not have to glaze it with ganache – a dusting of cocoa or icing sugar is perfectly elegant.

Preheat the oven to 180°C/fan 160°C/350°F/Gas 4. Butter the cake tin, line the base with baking parchment and butter the base and sides. Dust with flour.

Put the cocoa in a small bowl with the hot water and vanilla, then wait a few minutes and mix with a small whisk.

Put the butter into the bowl of a stand mixer and beat until pale. Add all but 50g of the sugar and beat again until the mixture is almost white. From time to time, scrape down the sides with a spatula. Beat in the egg yolks, followed by the (cooled) cocoa mixture and almonds. Continue to beat – the mixture will turn slightly paler as it is aerated.

Put the egg whites into a separate bowl and whisk with the salt until foamy. Add the cream of tartar, to set the foam, and then whisk until soft, white peaks of foam are formed. Add the remaining sugar then whisk until the peaks of foam are firm. Stir one large heaped tablespoon of the egg white into the cake mixture to loosen it, then fold in the rest with a large balloon whisk (the whisk on the stand mixer is ideal). By dipping the whisk slowly through the mixture, you will not disturb the air in it too much.

Pour the mixture into the prepared tin and gently spread it out to the edges using a palette knife. Bake the cake for 50–65 minutes. It will rise up but then fall again – even sink a little. Place the serving plate or board on top of the cake and invert.

To make the ganache, heat the cream in a small saucepan until nearly boiling. Remove from the heat and add the grated chocolate. Leave for 10 minutes then stir until glossy and smooth. Let it cool a little more until the glaze coats the back of a spoon thickly, then pour over the centre of the cake. If you like, you can decorate the cake with rose petals and flecks of gold leaf, for added glamour.

RICH FRUIT CAKE

Serves: 8

Equipment: *20cm cake tin with loose base*

Serving dish: *flat plate or cake stand*

125g butter, plus extra for greasing the tin

plain flour, for dusting the tin

125g golden syrup

125g soft dark brown sugar

85g softened prunes, halved

85g raisins

85g sultanas

1 tsp mixed spice

1 tsp cinnamon

2 eggs, beaten

1 small dessert apple, grated

250g ground almonds

To serve (optional):

apricot jam or marmalade, to glaze

candied fruits or edible gold leaf, to decorate

An easy-to-make, soggy, fruit-packed cake that will keep in a container for ages; ideal for covering with a layer of marzipan or rolled fondant icing.

Preheat the oven to 150°C/fan 130°C/300°F/Gas 2. Butter the tin, line the base with baking parchment, butter again then dust with flour.

Put the syrup, sugar, butter and dried fruit in a pan. Allow the butter to melt, bring to the boil and boil – not too hard – for 3 minutes. Remove from the heat and allow to cool for about 10 minutes. Add the spices and beat in the eggs. Stir in the grated apple and ground almonds and transfer to the cake tin. Bake for 1¾–2 hours. The cake will rise a little but not much. To test for doneness, insert a skewer into the centre and, if it comes out clean, the cake is ready. Allow to cool in the tin.

This cake can be glazed with apricot jam or marmalade that has been boiled and sieved. Decorate with candied fruits or possibly some gold leaf for Christmas.

Option: After glazing, you could cut a disk of marzipan and/or fondant icing to place over the surface of the cake.

VICTORIA SANDWICH STRAWBERRY CAKE

Serves 20

Equipment: *2x 30cm round tins; 2x 20cm round tins; 2x 10cm round tins (preferably all with loose bases)*

Serving dish: *board or cake stand*

For the first cake:

6 eggs, plus their weight in soft unsalted butter, white caster sugar and self-raising flour

3 tbsp milk

1 tsp vanilla extract

For the second cake:

4 eggs, plus their weight in soft unsalted butter, white caster sugar and self-raising flour

2 tbsp milk

½ tsp vanilla extract

For the third cake:

2 eggs, plus their weight in soft unsalted butter, white caster sugar and self-raising flour

To fill and decorate:

600g strawberry jam

600ml double cream, whipped until thick, or buttercream

icing sugar, for dusting

2kg strawberries, half sliced, half left whole

I made this three-layer cake for the wedding of my friends Bill and Tania. Naked but for icing sugar, filled very simply with jam, fresh berries and cream (or buttercream) then piled into layers and scattered with more fruit, it was homely and simple while celebratory. You can scale the size up and down to suit the number. The sponge can be made in advance, then frozen before assembly. I recommend using French or Danish unsalted butter, because it makes a lighter Victoria sponge. This butter is made with the lactic method, and is more stable when whisked at high speed. Occasionally, Victoria sponge batter curdles – it does not matter but the finished sponge will be a little heavier.

Preheat the oven to 160°C/fan 140°C/325°F/Gas 3. Generously butter your cake tins, then dust with flour and cover the base only with baking parchment.

This recipe is made in three batches. Put the eggs, butter, sugar, flour, milk and vanilla extract for the first cake in a mixer and beat until increased in volume and the batter becomes paler in colour. This may take 2–4 minutes.

Spoon the cake batter evenly into the larger prepared tins, spreading very lightly with a palette knife. Bake for 25–35 minutes until the surface feels springy. Insert a skewer into the cake and, if it comes out clean, the cake is done. Run a knife around the edge of the sponges and immediately turn out onto a rack to cool.

Repeat with the second and third cake, using the smaller prepared tins. Allow all to cool completely. If the cakes are very domed, you might have to level them with a knife (the garden birds or ducks will thank you). When assembling each 'sandwich', make sure that the top of the cake is innermost so the sponge bases, which are dead flat, form the surfaces.

Spread a layer of jam on 1 of each sized sponge and top with a ⅓ of the sliced strawberries. Spread cream or buttercream on the other sponges. Sandwich the jam and cream sponges together.

Spread a little jam on top of the larger sandwich, in the centre, then place the middle-sized sandwich on top. Repeat with the middle- and smallest-sized sponges. Place on a board or stand. Dust the whole cake with icing sugar, tilting it so that the sides are dusted too. Decorate with the whole strawberries – they look pretty cascading down the cake. If available, also use some on the stalk with leaves.

Options: Alpine strawberries from the garden look wonderful on this cake. Adapt to other berries or a mixture.

SIMPLE YEAST BREAD OR ROLLS

Makes 2 loaves (about 750g each) or 20 x 75g rolls

Equipment: two 20 x 10cm loaf tins or a flat baking sheet, lined with baking parchment

1kg strong white flour, plus extra for dusting

30g softened butter, or 2 tbsp olive oil

7g dried yeast or 15g fresh yeast

10g salt

650ml lukewarm water

This is a master recipe – you can use wholemeal or granary wheat flour, or a mix of flours – though it will not work with gluten-free flours. Add chopped woody herbs like rosemary or thyme, or toasted walnuts, if you wish. This bread keeps well for 2 days, and is good for toast for a further 2 days.

Put the flour in a large bowl and rub in the butter or oil. Add the yeast and salt and mix to distribute evenly. Pour in the water and mix with your hands or a wooden spoon to a lumpy dough. Turn the dough out on the floured worktop and knead for about 10 minutes – breaking now and again to allow it to relax before kneading again. You can do all of this in a stand mixer fitted with a dough hook.

Put the dough into the mixing bowl. Cover with clingfilm and leave in a warm place for 1½–2 hours until doubled in size.

Remove the dough from the bowl and knead to punch out the air. Cut into two and press each out into an oblong about 20cm wide to fit the tin. Put the dough in the tins and leave to prove in a warm place, uncovered, for about 30 minutes until well risen.

If making rolls, divide the dough into 20 pieces (you can weigh them if you want to be very precise). Using the cup of your hand and without too much flour on the worktop, roll in a circular motion until you have a smooth ball. Place the rolls on the baking sheet about 2cm apart. They will stick together in a batch as they rise – about 20 minutes.

Preheat the oven to 240°C/fan 220°C/475°F/Gas 9. Score the loaves or rolls with a blade about 5mm deep then bake until golden brown (turning the oven down to 200°C/fan 180°C/400°F/Gas 6 after 5 minutes). Bake for about 12 minutes for rolls, 30 minutes for loaves. Serve the rolls warm but the loaves will need to cool before slicing.

CORNBREAD

Makes 1 loaf (about 600g)

Equipment: *20cm round or square tin, lined with baking parchment*

235g cornmeal or polenta grains

200g plain flour

¾ tsp bicarbonate of soda

1 tsp salt

50g light brown sugar

3 eggs

390ml plain whole-milk yoghurt or buttermilk

30g butter, melted

This is lovely bread to serve with soup, barbecued meat or cassoulet (see page 90), and very easy to make. You can flavour it with crisp shards of smoked streaky bacon, or lightly with cheese.

Preheat the oven to 180°C/fan 160°C/350°F/Gas 4. Mix together the cornmeal, flour, bicarbonate of soda, salt and sugar. Beat in the eggs, yoghurt and melted butter then turn into the tin and bake for 20 minutes. Turn the heat down to 160°C/fan 140°C/325°F/Gas 3 for a further 20 minutes. Turn out onto a rack and allow to cool.

YEAST FLATBREADS

Makes 8 breads

540g strong white flour, plus extra for dusting

½ tsp salt

14g easy-bake yeast

150ml lukewarm whole milk (or yoghurt if making naan-style breads)

200ml lukewarm water

2 tbsp olive oil (or melted butter for naan) – for brushing

This recipe is adaptable, making both naan-type breads, pizza dough or flatbreads to wrap around grilled meat or feta cheese with herbs. The addition of yeast and also milk gives these breads a silky softness. If you make them the day before, wrap in foil and reheat the following day. You can also make the dough the evening before, put it in a large plastic container with the lid on, then refrigerate it. It will rise very slowly, which is good for the flavour and texture of the breads. About 2–3 hours before you eat, take it out of the fridge and allow it to come to room temperature before shaping it into balls.

Combine all the ingredients except the olive oil or butter and knead for several minutes until you have a smooth, tacky dough. Put in a large bowl, cover with clingfilm and leave to rise for 1½–2 hours, or until the dough has doubled in size. Divide the dough into 8 pieces and use a cupped hand to shape each into a ball, rolling them in circles on the floured worktop. When smooth and round, place the balls 10cm apart on a floured surface, dust the tops with flour and cover with sheets of clingfilm to prevent the surface of the dough becoming dry. Leave for 20 minutes until puffed and risen.

There are various ways to cook these breads: in the oven (220°C/fan 200°C/425°F/Gas 7) on a baking sheet lined with baking parchment to prevent sticking, or in the oven on a pizza 'stone'. Alternatively, cook them on the hob using a preheated, heavy-based flat griddle or pan. If you have an Aga, you can cook the breads directly on the right-hand hotplate.

Pick up one of the flatbreads and use both hands to gently stretch, without tearing it, into a thin oval. For naan, stretch it into a long, thin tear shape. Lay the bread in the pan. Cook until it swells and browns lightly on the underneath. Turn it and cook the other side. Brush the surface with the oil or melted butter, then turn it again. Brush again, then turn and allow to cook for another half minute, no more. When the bread feels springy if pressed, it is ready. Allow to cool wrapped in a cloth.

Options: For the following recipes, stretch the dough balls into a disc first. All the following recipes must be baked in the oven.

Baked rosemary-potato breads: cover the breads with new potato cut very thin on a mandolin, brush with olive oil then scatter over rosemary leaves and salt. Bake for 15–20 minutes at 200°C/fan 180°C/400°F/Gas 6.

Tomato breads: scatter halved cherry tomatoes over the surface of the breads. Sprinkle with oregano and olive oil and bake for 15–20 minutes at 200°C/fan 180°C/400°F/Gas 6.

Parcel breads: place 2 tbsp crumbled feta cheese in the centre of each bread, with 1 tbsp each chopped fresh mint, dill and parsley. Add 1 tbsp olive oil and freshly ground black pepper. Fold into a half-moon, sealing the edges by brushing with water. Sprinkle the breads with flour and bake for 15–20 minutes at 220°C/fan 200°C/425°F/Gas 7.

Coconut-coriander breads: scatter freshly grated coconut in the centre of each bread disc. Add 1–2 chopped green chillies, 1 tbsp chopped coriander, 1 tsp nigella seeds and a large pinch of cumin. Fold into a half-moon and seal by brushing the edges with water. Bake for 15–20 minutes at 220°C/fan 200°C/425°F/Gas 7 then, just before serving, brush the breads with melted butter.

BRIOCHE

Makes 2 large loaves (about 500g each)

Equipment: stand mixer fitted with a dough hook; two 20 x 10cm loaf tins, lined with baking parchment

350g unsalted butter, cold from the fridge

500g plain flour, plus extra for dusting

1 level tsp fine salt

7g dried yeast or 15g fresh yeast

60ml whole milk, at room temperature

1 level tbsp caster sugar

4 medium eggs, beaten, at room temperature

For the egg wash:

1 egg beaten with 1 tbsp sugar and a pinch of salt

Brioche is easier to make using an electric mixer. If you do make the dough by hand, keep all the ingredients cool and do the mixing in stages so the dough relaxes and stays cool and stable. Brioche freezes well.

Place the butter between two sheets of greaseproof paper and bash with a rolling pin until flattened to 1cm thick. Peel away the top sheet of paper, cut into 1cm dice, wrap and put back in the fridge.

Put the flour in the mixing bowl and add the salt and yeast. Mix briefly (use the beater attachment). Add the milk, sugar and eggs and mix at a low speed for approximately 10 minutes; the dough will be dry at first then become wetter.

Keeping the mixer on 'slow', add the butter dice, a few at a time, a few seconds apart so they are incorporated into the dough. You may find it takes a while for the cold butter to break down and become incorporated, and you may need to stop the mixer from time to time and scrape down the sides with a spatula.

Once all the butter has been added, mix for another 10 minutes at a higher speed. The mixture will become increasingly elastic and glossy. Turn off the mixer, scrape down the sides of the bowl, cover it with clingfilm and leave at room temperature for approximately 2 hours or until risen to double its size.

Preheat the oven to 200°C/fan 180°C/400°F/Gas 6. Scoop the dough out onto a floured worktop and divide in two. With floured hands, roughly shape each piece into a roll to fit the prepared tins. Brush the surface generously with the egg wash. Place one in each tin then bake for 25–30 minutes until risen and golden. Remove from the tins, place in the oven for 5 minutes on a baking tray, to crisp all the edges and ensure the brioches are fully cooked. They should feel lighter in weight.

PASTRY

If you make your own pastry, it has to far surpass anything that you can buy because it is something of a bother to make the first time – easy with a bit of practice, though. You can buy ready-made butter pastry in supermarkets and it is fine as a substitute for homemade, though never quite as crumbly or naturally delicious. I do know a source of artisan pastry, made with good butter and flour, and it is available via home delivery – see the Directory on page 268.

If you are going to make pastry, you need the best recipes for the basics: rough puff and shortcrust pastry. Rough puff is the easier, speedy-to-make version of puff pastry and, in my opinion, superior in its buttery-ness and the way it melts in the mouth. A savoury shortcrust pastry that rolls out to a thin, almost transparent casing is an essential recipe for bakers. See the next few pages.

ROUGH PUFF PASTRY

Makes 1kg pastry (enough for three 20 x 30cm flat sheets for tarts)

500g unsalted butter
500g plain flour, plus extra
    for dusting
250ml ice-cold water

One word of caution – when you first make this pastry you will think that the water quantity is too low because the dough will not immediately come together. Do not add extra, however, because the pastry will be impossible to work with later. The dough will eventually become smooth with the quantity allowed, I promise.

Put the butter between two sheets of greaseproof paper and tap hard with a rolling pin to soften. Put all the flour in a heap on the work surface, make a well in the centre and add the butter. Use your fingers to partially rub the butter into the flour, just to flatten the pieces, keeping them large, not to break them up further at this stage.

Add the water and form into a dryish dough; it will look crusty at the edges and there will be loose flour, but do not try to incorporate it at this stage – and don't add any more water. Wrap the piece of dough in greaseproof paper and put in the fridge for 15 minutes.

Clean the work surface using a dough scraper and dust it with a little flour. Take the dough from the fridge and unwrap it. Swiftly roll it into a rectangle, about 20 x 40cm. Fold it into three, like a letter (bring one third to the centre, then bring over the opposite third of pastry to lie on top of the fold). Tap it with a rolling pin, turn it 90 degrees, then roll out again to 20 x 40cm, making sure that it is not sticking and there is enough flour on the worktop.

Repeat this process a second time – fold, tap with the rolling pin – then wrap and refrigerate again, for 30 minutes. The pastry should by now have absorbed the dry and floury bits. Marbled lumps of butter will be visible inside the dough. Occasionally, a lump of butter breaks through – just dust the area with flour if this happens.

Repeat the rolling, folding and tapping one last time and refrigerate for at least 30 minutes before using the pastry.

TO USE THE PASTRY:

Roll out to about 5mm thickness. It can then be used for flat tarts. You can also use this pastry to make savoury nibbles to serve with drinks.

- Lay pickled anchovies on the pastry, with olives; bake until golden (at 200°C/fan 180°C/400°F/Gas 6) then cut into fingers.

- Grate Parmesan or another cheese onto the surface of the pastry; bake until golden at 200°C/fan 180°C/400°F/Gas 6.

- Spread anchovy paste, 'nduja or simply a mix of herbs with tomato purée onto the surface of the rolled-out pastry then roll it up. Chill then slice into round 'wheels'. Bake until golden at 200°C/fan 180°C/400°F/Gas 6.

SHORTCRUST PASTRY

Makes approximately 700g pastry (enough for at least 2 tarts, to cover 2 pies; 24 mince pies or 8 pasties)

1 tsp salt

375g plain flour, plus extra for dusting

250g diced butter

75ml (5 tbsp) ice-cold water, or more

A fail-safe, quite buttery shortcrust that is ideal for lining tins, covering pies or making pasties. It is very easy to handle and can be rolled very thin – which is a requirement for tarts because I hate biting into thick and therefore usually undercooked pastry.

Sieve the salt and flour together in a large bowl, add the butter and mix to a breadcrumb stage. This can be done in a stand mixer using the dough hook or food processor. Add the water and mix until it comes together as a dough.

At this stage, pinch a little bit of the dough between your thumb and index finger. It should not crumble or break apart (too dry), or feel too soft so your digits meet (too wet) but when pressed feel smooth and malleable with some resistance. Add a little water (if dry) or flour (if wet), lightly kneading it into the dough.

Take the dough out of the mixing bowl and knead on a very lightly floured worktop until it is smooth. Form into an oblong tablet (easier when it comes to dividing for use later), wrap in clingfilm and rest in fridge for at least 20 minutes before using. It will store in the fridge for 24 hours, or in the freezer for up to 2 weeks if frozen when very fresh.

ROLLING THE PASTRY INTO A CIRCLE FOR A TART:

Remove the pastry from the fridge and leave for 30 minutes to soften slightly. Dust the worktop with flour. Cut the quantity of pastry you need and place it on the worktop. Tap the pastry all over the surface with the rolling pin to flatten it a little, then begin to roll, making a swift, even movement back and forth.

So you end up with an even circle, turn the pastry 30 degrees and roll back and forth once again. Check there is enough flour dusted under the pastry and add a little more if it is beginning to stick. Continue to roll in this way until you have a circle the size of a dinner plate. It will become too difficult to turn the pastry each time from now on, so (checking it is not sticking) adjust the angle and roll it into a perfect circle, 2.5mm thick.

TO MAKE A BLIND-BAKED (EMPTY) TART CASE
WITH SAVOURY PASTRY:

Preheat the oven to 180°C/fan 160°C/350°F/Gas 4. You do not need to butter the tart tin. Pick up the pastry by wrapping it around the rolling pin then drape it loosely across the tin. Ease the pastry down the sides, making sure it is well tucked into the corners. Press it up against the sides and allow the extra to hang over the top edge. Do not trim it but bake it this way. It will be trimmed after baking.

Prick the base of the pastry a few times, to prevent it lifting during cooking. To make sure this does not happen, place a sheet of greaseproof paper inside the tart and half-fill with baking beans.

Bake for about 20 minutes, until the pastry is dry under the beans, but not brown. Take the tart out of the oven and turn it down to 160°C/fan 140°C/325°F/Gas 3, remove the paper lining and beans and return to crisp the pastry base a little more.

The pastry case is now ready to use. If any cracks appear during cooking, patch them with spare pastry, stuck on with water. Bake for 5 minutes to secure the patches. If you are making a pastry case for a liquid mixture, such beaten eggs and milk for a cheese tart, brush the inside of the blind-baked pastry case with beaten egg and return to the oven to harden.

This pastry case can be frozen in advance of being used, and will keep in an airtight container for 3 days.

PARTY

CHEESE

20–50 people

A board or table, in its middle a whole cheese, handmade with the rough outer rind dusted with white and charcoal grey spores; beside it chunks of sourdough bread or tender, nubbly biscuits made of oatmeal or other grains, a bowl of sticky sharp chutney or pickle and some fruit. There are two or three other entire and very tempting cheeses on the table: a younger fresh type with a chalky, crinkly rind and another, enclosed in a balsawood box, oozes pungently. A cheese table is a very beautiful meal but it is also an answer. The question being: how do you throw a party for a large number which looks and tastes wonderful, and feeds hungry people properly, effortlessly and elegantly?

Another generation called such events cheese and wine parties. Admittedly, these parties gained a bad reputation, with offerings of Edam cut into triangles served alongside a plate of stick-to-the-roof-of-the-mouth water biscuits. But this was before the revival of interest in artisan ingredients, especially the comeback of British farmhouse cheeses. Essentially, these cheeses are now widely available and this transforms the cheese party, dragging it into a new era, in an exciting way. The cheeses to discover are myriad – see the directory for suppliers (page 270).

At a party like this, you do not need to hand anything around. If people

are hungry, they will migrate towards the table and food. They will make a mess, but in this instance there is nothing offensive about cheeses being enthusiastically dug into, crumbs scattered, or drips of chutney – it is a happy and relaxed way to offer food.

If anything, the only skills needed are making good choices with regard to shopping (see 'choosing cheese', page 176) then putting the table together with some flair. Set the scene with a good surface or background. You can buy large wooden boards, but they can be expensive. If you have time in the run-up to the party, order a one-metre piece of beech kitchen counter – this is easy and inexpensive online. You will need to spend a couple of hours one day or evening sanding it, then use a cloth to rub olive oil into the wood. This is the glossy, natural 'canvas' onto which you can work with your good things, putting a cheese here, a bowl of chutney or honey there, scattering some plums or pears. Feel free to be creative and, again, if you have that bit of extra time, add to the effect with the homemade oatcakes (page 177), chutney or roasted grapes (see pages 178–179).

It will take approximately one hour to set up.

You will need plenty of knives for cutting cheese, spoons for runny cheese. Saucer and spoon, tongs for pots/bowls of pickle and chutney, jellies or honey. If the surface space is small, use an elevated cake stand or two to create more room.

CHOOSING CHEESE

Choose the best handmade cheeses for your table (see Directory, page 270). Block Cheddar is a good everyday cheese but this is a party. Offer at least three cheeses – working on the basis of one hard, one soft, one strong, i.e. blue-veined or a cheese with washed rind. If you are a large number, several different cheeses create interest and look great. It is a matter of finding something for all tastes, so choose cheeses that are interesting to you but that complement each other – and, essentially, that you think others will like. Some cheeses are naturally small, like young goat's cheeses, so buy a few of them and group them on the table. Very fresh cheeses can be rolled in chopped fresh herbs and presented on a plate or, if available, put them on an edible leaf – fig or vine leaves are ideal, and very pretty.

I find it easiest to choose a cheese menu, or combination, by texture. If buying generic cheeses like cheddar, Wensleydale or brie, choose artisan types, handmade on the farm, not a factory.

SOFT CHEESES

Bloomy rind – Camembert, Brie de Meaux, Wigmore, Waterloo, St James, Mileen or Tunworth.

Fresh goat's cheese – plain crotins, St Tola, Trickle or Ragstone; dusted with ash, e.g. Dorstone, Golden Cross, St Maur or Monte Enebro.

Creamy – Chaource, Delice de Bourgogne , la Tur, Winslade

Washed rind – Stinking Bishop, Adlestrop, Roblochon, Munster

SEMI-SOFT CHEESES

Single Gloucester, Yarg, Rachel, Tomme de Savoie, Ardrahan, Old Smales, Durrus, Sharpham Rustic, Duckett's Caerphilly, Richard III Wensleydale, Appelby Cheshire, Gubbeen, Tickelmore, Morn Dew, Curworthy, Devon Oake, Perl Las

HARD CHEESES

Farmhouse cheddar, either Daylesford, Montgomery, Keens or other from West Country producer group; Gruyère, Emmental, Coolea, St Gall, Gouda, Mimolette, Daylesford Double Gloucester

BLUE CHEESES

Stichelton, Colston Basset Stilton, Dorset Blue Vinney, Bledington Blue, Beenleigh Blue, Bath Blue, Barkham Blue, Gorgonzola, Dolcelatte, Fourme d'Ambert

HOMEMADE FRUITY OATCAKES

Makes about 60

450g fine oatmeal, plus extra
  for dusting
small pinch of baking
  powder
180g softened butter, cubed
120g raisins, chopped into
  small pieces
1 tsp sea salt
2 eggs, beaten

Rich oatcakes with a buttery taste, which, with the added chopped raisins, are slightly chewy. You can add or substitute other seeds and grains, if you wish, but not too many or the biscuits will break easily. If you do not have time to make your own biscuits there are many excellent artisan biscuits available (see Directory, page 268).

Preheat the oven to 180°C/fan 160°C/350°F/Gas 4 and line 2 baking sheets with baking parchment (you will have to work in batches.).

Put the oatmeal and baking powder in a large bowl. Rub in the butter, stir in the chopped raisins, salt and eggs and mix to a dough. Dust a work surface with fine oatmeal and roll the dough out until about 5mm thick. It can be sticky, which is good for the richness of the oatcakes but makes it tricky to handle.

Use a round cutter (or a variety of shaped cutters) to cut out the oatcakes. Lift them off the worktop carefully with a palette knife or spatula and place on the baking sheet. Shape the surplus dough into a ball and repeat the rolling process until you have used up every scrap. Bake for about 8–12 minutes, until pale gold. Leave on the baking sheet for a few minutes then transfer to a rack to cool. They will crisp up as they cool down.

OLIVE AND FIG PICKLE

Makes 2 large jars, 750g capacity (enough for a party of 30–40 people)

600g pitted kalamata olives
200ml balsamic vinegar
100ml water
240g soft brown sugar
400g dried figs, halved
  and sliced

Dark and shining, with earthy sweet-sourness, this pickle goes with all cheeses and is very quick and uncomplicated to make. Use natural black olives and not the budget type that have the additive ferrous gluconate, which has an unpleasant iron flavour. Kalamata are best, and not too expensive.

Drain then roughly chop the olives and put them in a saucepan with all the other ingredients. Bring to the boil and simmer for about 15 minutes. If the mixture is too dry, add a little more water. The balance of sweet-sour will depend on how sweet the figs are, so you may need to adjust the flavours. Taste the pickle and, if too sweet, add a little more balsamic vinegar; add a little extra sugar if too sour. Transfer to sterilised jars and store.

SCENTED HONEY

Makes 450g

450g runny honey
3 sprigs thyme
1 sprig rosemary

Honey tastes wonderful with soft and fresh cheeses, and I am sure you know the flavour of all honey is influenced by the different pollens gathered by the bees that make it. But you can add another layer of aroma to runny honey, by infusing it with woody herbs, in this case thyme and rosemary. It looks pretty, too. Honey flavoured with truffles, available from Italian food shops, is also delicious with cheese, especially mature cheddar or pecorino.

Bruise the herbs by tapping the sprigs with a wooden spoon while on a board. Put the sprigs into the jar and leave to infuse for an hour or two.

ROAST GRAPES

Makes 1.5kg

1.5kg red grapes
2 tbsp extra virgin olive oil
2 pinches of salt

My friend the food writer Skye McAlpine once served these with roast duck, for dinner. Ordinary red grapes take on a beautiful colour when roasted, and ooze sweet juice. Guests can pick off a grape to eat with biscuits and cheese – very delicious. Bunches, roasted and glossy, are an appetising central focus on a cheese board or table.

Preheat the grill. Brush the grapes with the oil, sprinkle over the salt and place in the oven, under the grill, or bake at 200c. Remove after 5–10 minutes when the grapes are blistered, but not browned.

Options: Replace the pickle with another or add to it – for example, the carrot pickle on page 32. Roast figs can replace or add to the roasted grapes.

TWO STAND UP DINNERS

40–60 people

Big party, small space, low budget, no one goes hungry – this has been the brief for those relaxed parties that might mark birthdays, engagements, anniversaries; hail Christmas; say 'thank you' or 'goodbye'; launch an idea, or just be a reason to get together. These parties, which my parents generation dubbed 'buffets', are put t'ogether quickly with little fuss, and we love them. They remind me of many happy, somewhat uncontrolled, admittedly messy parties where guests appeared to be jammed in every corner of our home.

Faced with the challenge, hosts – understandably – head off to buy nuts, olives and crisps hoping that a fast-flowing drink supply and jolly company will compensate for the lack of supper. Supper is possible, however, within limitations. The following two parties are based on those we held in our south London home and I have continued to serve these menus ever since because they work so well. They have a vague theme, though are mainly chosen for reasons of practicality. Both suit numbers of between forty and sixty, though you could do the duck and barley menu for up to a hundred.

The recipes over the following pages can be scaled down for smaller numbers, even to serve just a few. Scaling down is usually common sense but you will find that a few guests eat more, especially when seated. Note that quantities of ingredients like rice or other grains are usually calculated at about 40–50g per head for small groups, and 30g per head for large groups.

PERSIAN FEAST

My birthday is three weeks exactly before Christmas, slap in the middle of the party season. We used to throw a party in our kitchen, starting at 7pm and going on until midnight. Some people came for an hour, some for the whole evening. I would do enough supper for a maximum of sixty, though more might pass through. We usually ran out of food by 9.30, perhaps 10, but that was acceptable. I hoped any latecomers would have eaten. Giving these parties taught me a lot. Big one-pot dishes that can be left to cool to room temperature worked the best. For a long time I was on the lookout for a recipe that had the 'everything factor': popular, delectable but a little offbeat – not a dish you might get at every party.

Duck and barley pilav has 'it', as do the accompanying flatbreads stuffed with fresh salty cheese and herbs. The pilav actually began life as a dish of pheasant and rice after I bought a job lot of pheasants from a game dealer. The two recipes have a lot in common. Onion cooked until sweet, a seasoning of allspice, cloves and orange; tenderly cooked meat, the richness of butter, freshness of soft green herbs with pomegranate seeds, dramatic as a broken ruby necklace, scattered across the surface. Aside from the obvious difference between the pheasant prototype and the recent duck incarnation (duck legs are available easily, all year round) is the use of pearled (polished) barley in place of rice. I find that the down-to-earth British grain is more appropriate in this recipe.

The flatbreads with cheese and herbs are not a recipe as such, more of a hand-held picnic suggestion. The cheese – a feta or similar – is crumbled and served in a bowl dressed with a little oil. I buy soft flatbreads from Middle Eastern shops – Iranian soft flatbreads are the best because they are very tender and need no reheating. I cut them into manageable sizes, and put a mixture of soft herbs beside them. All the guests need to do is spoon some of the cheese on a sheet of bread, add herbs and wrap it.

SLOW-ROASTED DUCK LEGS
with spiced barley
Serves: 40–60

Serving dish: large platters

For the slow-roasted duck:

45 duck legs, pricked with
    a skewer then seasoned
    with salt and freshly
    ground black pepper

200g duck fat

2 tsp ground cloves

2 tbsp ground coriander

1 tbsp ground black pepper

zest of 5 oranges

For the barley:

16 medium brown onions,
    finely chopped

18 garlic cloves, 10 chopped
    and 8 sliced

200ml olive oil

1.5 kg pearl barley

5 tsp ground allspice

1.5kg butter

6 litres water or stock, and
    more

salt and freshly ground black
    pepper

To serve:

500g flat-leaf parsley,
    chopped

3 pomegranates, pips only

2 litres Greek yoghurt

*The duck, onion and barley can be prepared in advance then warmed together in
a pan before serving, making this an easy dish for large parties. Palm leaf plates or
small bowls are ideal for guests to dish the food into, with cornstarch spoons – both
are disposable – see Directory, page 272.*

Preheat the oven to 160°C/fan 140°C/325°F/Gas 3. Put the duck legs in a
casserole with the duck fat and spices and orange zest. Brown quickly then
put in roasting trays. Roast slowly for 1½ hours until the meat is very tender
and falling off the bone. Set aside to cool then take all the meat off the bone.
If the skin is not crisp, place it back in the oven, turning up the heat and roast
until crisp. Remove it from the oven and chop into small pieces. Set to one
side.

Meanwhile, cook the onions and chopped garlic cloves in a large pan with
the oil over a low-medium heat until they are golden and sweet. If you do not
have a very large pan, do this in batches. Lift the cooked onions out of the pan
with a slotted spoon, leaving behind as much oil as possible. Discard the oil.

Put the barley in the pan with the sliced garlic, allspice and butter, and fry
for a few minutes. Add water or stock to cover by about 10cm then bring to
the boil and simmer for about 25 minutes until the barley is cooked al dente.
Season to taste with salt and black pepper then mix in the onions and set
aside in a warm place.

Before serving: Reheat the duck and skin in a frying pan – you will not need
oil. Season it to taste with more salt, if necessary.

To serve, heap the barley onto a serving dish then the duck on top. Scatter
over the parsley and the pomegranate pips. Put bowls of yoghurt on the table,
with spoons.

FLATBREADS

with herbs and fresh cheese

Serves 40–60

Serving dish: large board or platter

20 large sheets of lavash
flatbread, cut into 20 ×
20cm squares, or 40–60
soft flat round breads

2kg fresh feta cheese

400ml extra virgin olive oil

3 large bunches dill

3 large bunches coriander

3 large bunches mint

Lebanese or Iranian lavash breads are ideal for wrapping around the cheese and herbs. Silky and very thin, they usually come in large, 40 x 30cm, rectangles and are sold in plastic bags to keep them fresh. Most cities have Middle Eastern bakeries and it is worth going to them for the freshest flatbreads. Lavash is also available online, but do contact the bakery or seller first to ask about freshness. They keep for at least 3–4 days in the bag but the sooner they are eaten the better. Ordinary wraps from supermarkets are a little bit thick, but if several are packed in foil and heated before use, they can be used in place of more authentic breads. Naans and chapattis are unsuitable as wraps.

If you are making a trip to buy the breads from a Middle Eastern shop, you may as well buy the feta cheese at the same time. Not only is the quality better, it is much cheaper as a bulk buy than the little 250g slabs sold in supermarkets. My favourite is made from a mix of ewe's and goat's milk and is sold in cans preserved in brine – but there is always a variety to choose from.

Put the flatbreads on a large board or plate and cover with a damp cloth so they do not dry out.

Crumble the feta cheese into a bowl and dress with the oil. Snip off any hard stalks from the herbs and place them beside the breads.

Assemble a few of the wraps, just so that guests can see what they have to do themselves: Put a tablespoonful of the cheese onto a square of bread, add some herbs and wrap it up tightly.

INDIAN FEAST

I enjoy making Indian-inspired food for parties. The colours are festive, the flavours exciting and it is hard to find a person who is not a devotee. Indian food serves both carnivores and vegetarians with egalitarian sympathy. No one feels left out. The sensual side notwithstanding, the practicalities of making and serving the meal win. Indian food lends itself to sharing between a large number, being filling, relatively inexpensive to make, and tandoori, curries and dal do not mind sitting around keeping warm.

Then there is the bread. Warm, soft and filling naan breads are a second spoon. And you do not need to make them, just the dishes to go with them. For one of our first parties, we placed a sort of staggered order with the curry house near our home. We were cooking for nearly sixty and the restaurant delivered three batches of 10 naans – partly because they could not bake more than four or five breads in their tandoor oven at once. The plan worked perfectly in tandem with the random arrival of guests through the evening. If you don't have a nearby supply, however, you can buy good-quality naans, sprinkle them with water, wrap them in foil and reheat them in a low oven.

The following recipes can be cooked individually to serve with dal and naan. The tandoori in this chapter is best done on a barbecue so is more suited to a party in summer. For the colder months there is the Coconut Chilli Chicken. Alternatively, the Kitchari can be served simply with naan. All go well together but if serving this feast, keep the numbers down to twenty people.

SPICED BARBECUED POUSSINS

Serves: 40–60

Equipment: skewers and large plastic bags for marinating the poussins

Serving dish: large wooden board or flat platter

20–30 poussins

For the first marinade:
600ml malt vinegar
3 tbsp ground turmeric
300g grated fresh ginger
12 tsp red chilli powder
3 garlic bulbs, cloves crushed

For the second marinade:
5 tbsp ground mace
3 tbsp ground cloves
3 tbsp ground star anise
8 tsp ground cumin
120ml vegetable oil
250g whole-milk or Greek yoghurt

To serve:
4 large bunches fresh coriander
4 large bunches fresh mint
black sesame or nigella seeds
plain whole-milk or Greek yoghurt

Perfect for summer, and a big barbecue. I love the flavour of mace, garlic and ginger in this marinade for chicken made very tender by the traditional use of malt vinegar. You can also use larger chickens, spatchcocked, as for the poussins, and the recipe can also be adapted for lamb, threaded onto skewers, or lamb chops.

To save time, ask your butcher to prepare the poussins for spatchcock, removing the skin and discarding it. To spatchcock the poussins turn each one over and snip along the backbone from the 'parson's nose' end. Turn the bird over and use your open palm to flatten it out, with the flesh uppermost. If the butcher hasn't already done so, remove as much of the skin as you possibly can – the legs can be difficult – then use a sharp knife to score the plumper parts of the flesh on breast and leg. This helps the marinade to penetrate the meat. To secure the spatchcock poussins, thread a skewer horizontally through legs and breast.

Mix together the ingredients for the first marinade and smear it all over the poussins, especially on the flesh side. The best way to do this is with your hands, wearing food-safe gloves. Place in strong plastic bags and refrigerate for 1 hour. Mix together all the ingredients for the second marinade, smear it over the chickens as before and then place back in the bags and marinate for at least 2 hours or up to 24 hours before cooking. The chickens must be refrigerated.

To cook the poussins in an oven, preheat the oven to 200°C/fan 180°C/400°F/ Gas 6, place them in roasting dishes lined with baking parchment and roast until golden and the meat thoroughly cooked – about 20–25 minutes. You will have to work in batches if cooking a large number. To barbecue, cook for approximately 20–25 minutes each side, or until the juices inside run clear, with no pink, when tested with a skewer. Once cooked, set the poussins aside in a warm place until ready to serve.

COCONUT CHILLI CHICKEN

Serves: 40–60

Serving dish: shallow pan or bowl

6kg boneless chicken thighs, diced

2kg whole-milk yoghurt

For the paste:

500g desiccated coconut

1 litre water

300ml sunflower oil

40 green cardamoms, ground

6 cinnamon sticks

4 tsp ground cloves

12 large shallots, thinly sliced

500g fresh ginger, peeled and grated

30 garlic cloves (3 bulbs), grated

12 tsp ground turmeric

6 tsp cayenne pepper

12 tsp smoked paprika

3kg plum tomatoes, chopped

24 green chillies, quartered lengthways and deseeded

6 × 450g cans coconut milk

salt, to taste

To serve:

large bunch fresh coriander leaves

fresh ginger, cut into thin matchsticks

A creamy, coconut-laden, mildly hot and satisfying curry that goes a long way and is especially warming for a winter party. You will need a large pan, which can be borrowed or hired but it is possible to buy big inexpensive pans from ethnic markets – they will be a good investment for future parties.

Combine the chicken with the yoghurt and leave to tenderise for 20 minutes. Put the coconut and half the water in a liquidiser and blend to a paste, as smooth as possible. Add the rest of the water, process again and set to one side.

Heat the oil and add the cardamoms, cinnamon and cloves, then add the shallots and cook over a low heat, gently sizzling, until they are pale gold in colour. Add the ginger, garlic, turmeric, cayenne pepper and smoked paprika. Cook for 1 minute then add the tomatoes and green chillies, cook for another minute then add the coconut paste. Simmer for about 5 minutes then add the chicken. Simmer slowly for about 15 minutes.

Finally, add the coconut milk and simmer for a few minutes. Taste and add a little salt if necessary. Serve with the fresh coriander and ginger matchsticks.

DAL
with butter and ginger

Serves: 40–60

Serving dish: large bowl or shallow pan

1.5kg hulled mung dal

7 tsp ground turmeric

24 small green chillies, split lengthways

500g butter

7 tsp cumin seeds

300g grated fresh ginger, plus 1cm piece, cut into matchsticks

12 tomatoes, deseeded and chopped

2–4 tsp asafoetida, to taste

salt, to taste

1 large bunch coriander, chopped

To serve:

30 naan breads, cut in half, wrapped in foil and kept warm in the oven

Dal, or spiced braised pulses, is the most economical food yet rich and filling. It should always be served with naan breads. The following recipe is one of the simplest but most delicious, made without onion or garlic and gently spiced. The tomatoes give it a fresh taste and the butter – essential – brings all the flavours together.

Wash the mung dal in a sieve held under the cold tap for 1 minute. Put them in a large pan, cover with plenty of water, add the turmeric and chillies and bring to the boil. If a lot of foam rises to the surface, skim it off and discard it. Boil the dal until it is tender, about 15–20 minutes, adding more water if necessary. Drain it in a sieve and set to one side.

Wash the pan and then place over the heat. Add the butter, cumin and ginger. Cook gently sizzling for 1 minute then add the tomatoes and asafoetida. Cook for another minute then add the dal. Cook for another 3 minutes then taste and add salt if necessary. Add a little more water if the dal is too thick – it should be quite soupy. Just before serving add the ginger matchsticks and coriander.

KITCHARI

Serves: 40–60

1.5kg basmati rice

3.6kg undyed smoked haddock

8 onions, sliced

36 cardamom pods, crushed

1.5 litres whole milk

750ml double cream

48 free-range eggs

6 tsp cumin seeds

48 fennel seeds

1½ tsp ground mace

1½ tsp cayenne pepper

150g piece fresh ginger, peeled and grated

400g butter, melted

salt and freshly ground black pepper

large bunch coriander, leaves only

Basmati and smoked haddock, with spiced cream and eggs. An easy dish for a large number, I have relied on this recipe for many years and it is as good hot as cold.

Put the rice in a large pan, cover with plenty of water, bring to the boil and simmer for about 10 minutes or until the rice is just cooked – not fluffy. Drain and then spread out on a serving dish. Cover with a clean tea towel.

Put the fish in a wide shallow frying pan and add the onions and cardamom pods. Pour over the milk and cream and heat until the milk mixture simmers. Cook very gently for about 5 minutes until the fish begins to flake. Remove from the heat. Transfer the fish to a plate. Pass the cream through a sieve, discard the onions and cardamoms, then set the liquid to one side. Flake the fish over the rice.

Boil the eggs, pricking the round end of each with a pin to prevent cracking then bringing to the boil and counting 5 minutes. Run under the cold tap to cool, then tap and peel them.

Clean the frying pan, then toast the cumin and fennel seeds together. If you have a pestle and mortar or spice grinder, pound them to a powder, but they can be left whole. Add the mace, cayenne pepper and ginger with the butter and fry gently over a low heat for 1 minute, to make a spicy paste. Add the cream then bring to simmering point. Taste and season with salt and black pepper. Pour this over the fish and rice and mix carefully. Cut the eggs in half and put on top. Scatter over the coriander and serve.

SUMMERTIME FEAST

60 people

A party for a large number, sitting down
to the meal, takes more planning than
any other. I am not going to say it is
easy but some of the best parties are put
together by families or groups of friends
and without professional help. If you
can stay within what is possible and
allow practicality to guide your choices,
you can create something lovely which,
importantly, you will also enjoy.

The party shown on these pages was
our own. It was a shared party, held
on a July evening, with a mix of our
friends and those of our children,
who celebrated their eighteenth and
twenty-first birthdays in the same year.
With a sit-down dinner, we entered a
completely new realm of hospitality, one
that needs a great deal more planning.
The main challenge was to keep the
cost low, choosing a menu and style that
the family, along with the help of a few
friends, could manage.

With dinners for large numbers it is
easy to understand why people are often
tempted to take the stress-free route and
pay for caterers and professional party
planners. Such parties, where every
detail is beautifully organised, make
wonderful memories, especially for very
significant occasions like weddings. I
think many brides – and their parents
for that matter – would rather take out a
bank loan than be their own caterer on
the big day. You can hardly blame them,
and yet group-effort parties still endure

and have all the charm of those that are meticulously planned.

There is one phrase to write large on the notebook that will carry all your to-do lists: Know Your Limitations. When it comes to food, choose recipes that are in your comfort zone. Most of us do not have the time or experience to make tray after tray of canapés – so avoid them altogether. The extent of your ambition should be this: throw a party in which you are a participant and not a slave.

It comes down to being very realistic. Firstly, accept the fact that something will not go according to plan. So you need to build in a contingency – at least a couple of hours spare before the party begins. Obviously, the key is to prepare as much as possible, well in advance. The syrup base for a cocktail or the pudding or cake, for example.

Next, accept every offer of help, and also ask for it. Your good friends and loved ones will want to help hand around food and drink and, just as importantly, help to clear.

The unknowns have to be known. Quite often we pick an easy-to-prepare recipe but do not take into account that it might take ages to serve. For example, if a main course requires carving or slicing, avoid it altogether. Choose instead dishes that can be placed on tables, to which guests can help themselves or help each other. Minimise the menu – an outstanding one-pot dish is as good as three courses – but be generous, offer plenty and more.

The party was in our own garden, so we needed cover. In July the nights can still be cool and dewy and yes, of course, it can rain. We found a tent measuring 12 x 18 metres/40–60 feet, big enough to fit eight tables seating eight people. We also rented chairs and tables. Outside I hung strings of rain-proof battery-operated LED lights, so no need for long cables. Two fire pits were lit, both borrowed from friends, and wheelbarrows formed mobile ice buckets. We used a dresser base for an outside bar. Our children and their friends did a great deal to help set up, some arriving early. You get nothing unless you ask, I muttered to myself, delighted. The lesson learned being that there is really no such thing as a hero when it comes to giving a party. You have to enjoy it, even if there is a rush beforehand – or a panic. So ask for and accept help – and, essentially, allow time to solve problems. At our July party, at the end of a very stormy week, these came in the form of a severely damaged tent that arrived late. It had been almost irretrievably damaged by the wind at a party two nights earlier. Two hours were spent stitching it together and, though it caused a last-minute rush, we were saved by having chosen a slow-cooked main course that had been prepared in advance. Had we chosen to barbecue the food, no one would have been fed before midnight.

Again, the nature of a family-style party means no need for smart china. All crockery, cutlery and glassware is available for hire, at a considerably high cost, but the alternative no longer means paper or plastic plates. There has been a green revolution in disposables in the form of plates of every size made from compressed palm leaves. They are nice to eat from and look natural. With the type of hand-held food on our menu, they could not have been more informally perfect. For drinks we hired glasses for wine, and used jam jars for cocktails.

ELDERFLOWER AND LIME MOJITOS

Makes 4 litres (enough for 60 people)

To serve: tumblers or jam jars, short cocktail straws

For the Elderflower and Lime cordial:

1.8kg golden caster sugar

3 litres water

12 limes

6 lemons

60 elderflower heads

For the Elderflower and Lime Mojitos (makes 10):

500ml dark rum (600ml if you are making a stronger punch)

300ml elderflower and lime cordial (see above)

10 small sprigs mint, leaves only

ice and soda water

Made a few weeks before the July party, elderflower and lime cordial would be the base of a rum punch to offer to arriving guests. Elder flowers in late May, early June and grows in hedgerows on roadsides.

Put the sugar in a large pan and pour over the water. Allow it to soak into the sugar and then place it over a low heat. Meanwhile, squeeze the limes and lemons, retaining the halves of the fruit. When the water reaches boiling point, add all the juice, the fruit halves and the elderflower. Leave to steep for 24 hours then strain, retaining the liquid. Pour into sterilised containers or bottles and store in the fridge.

Mix together the rum and cordial. Put the mint on a chopping board and bruise it with a rolling pin or wooden spoon – this is easier when making several drinks at once. Divide the mint among tumblers or jam jars, then half-fill them with ice. Add 80ml of the rum-cordial mix to each glass then top up with soda water. Serve with a cocktail straw.

CHAR CEVICHE

with lime, sesame and fresh wasabi

Serves: 15

Serving dish: individual bowls
or large bowls to place on
tables for people to help
themselves

1kg boneless, skinless fillet
  of char (or cod, bream or
  sea bass)
juice of 4 limes
juice of 2 lemons

For the dressing:
juice of 4 limes (2 tbsp)
4 tbsp light soy sauce
2 tbsp Thai fish sauce
1 tbsp maple syrup

To serve:
3 tbsp toasted sesame oil
2 mild green chillies, halved,
  de-seeded and chopped
4 tbsp baby leaves or micro
  leaves (radish, perilla,
  mizuna, rocket)
1–2 tbsp Thai dried shrimps,
  ground (optional), or sea
  salt
5cm piece fresh wasabi (one
  root) or horseradish

*Char is a cousin of salmon, with denser, white-pink flesh. The Peruvian method of
'cooking' fish in citrus suits it perfectly but cod, bream or sea bass could also be used.
To buy char, see the Directory page 269.*

*By extraordinary coincidence, with char also being ideal sashimi fish (raw, to eat
Japanese style or use to make sushi), we also live near a farm producing wasabi
and added it to our multicultural ceviche. Fresh wasabi is expensive, but a little
goes a long way. I also added a little ground dried shrimp, which acts as a powerful
seasoning. If you feel this is a little much, use sea salt. For our party of sixty, I served
the ceviche in small palm leaf bowls, with forks, to eat before sitting down.*

Cut the fish lengthways into 2–3 strips, depending on the thickness of the
fillet. Then slice thinly, about 2–3mm, across the grain of the flesh. Place in
a non-corrosive bowl, then pour over the lime and lemon juice and mix well.
Place the bowl in the fridge for approximately 15 minutes, until the fish has
lost its translucence and appears to be 'cooked'. Transfer the fish to a colander
set over a bowl and allow all the surplus juice to drain away – then discard
the juice.

Combine all the dressing ingredients in a bowl. To serve, transfer the fish to
a serving dish. Pour the dressing, in a thin dribble, back and forth to cover the
fish. Do not stir it, however. Then do the same with the sesame oil, and scatter
over the green chillies and leaves. Sprinkle with the ground dried shrimp (if
using), or scrunch over a couple of pinches of sea salt. Then grate or shave
the wasabi or horseradish directly onto the ceviche.

Serve a single tablespoonful to each guest in a small bowl or plate, with a
fork.

Important: Prepare the ceviche within 4 hours of eating; no more or the fish
will be overwhelmed by the flavour of the citrus and will deteriorate.

MARINATED SLOW-COOKED LAMB SHOULDER
with roast fennel, garlic sauce and flatbreads
Each 2kg lamb shoulder serves 8–10

Serving dish: Shallow platters

1 large lamb shoulder
(2kg, on the bone)
Olive oil
100ml white wine
100ml water

For the marinade:

4 tbsp olive oil
4 garlic cloves, chopped or
grated
2 tbsp fresh rosemary leaves,
finely chopped
1 tbsp fresh thyme leaves,
chopped
juice of 1 lemon
1 tbsp ground coriander
seeds
1 tbsp ground black pepper
2 tsp fennel seeds

**For the fennel and garlic
sauce:**

2 fennel bulbs
1 tbsp vegetable oil
4 garlic cloves, crushed
2 tbsp tahini
juice of 1 lemon
150ml Greek yoghurt
sea salt
1 tbsp mint leaves, to serve

*Slow-cooked lamb shoulder is ideal big party food, being economical and easy to
serve – it does not need carving because the meat falls off the bone when fully cooked.
The meat, without the bone, can then be served at the table simply with a spoon and
fork. It can also be prepared in advance, taken off the bone and reheated for serving.
We marinated it for 24 hours two days before the party, cooked it earlier in the day
then left it covered with foil, ready to be reheated.*

*The best flatbread to use is soft, thin lavash, which does not need reheating, available
from Middle Eastern bakeries and online. If using thicker tortillas, test out various
types from different supermarkets or bakeries before the event, so you know the best
source. Refresh them by heating in batches of eight, wrapped in foil.*

Mix together the marinade ingredients and rub all over the lamb. Put the
lamb in a strong plastic bag, or two bags, and place it in the fridge. If you are
preparing several lamb shoulders for a large party, putting the lamb shoulders
into bags takes up less fridge space. Marinate the lamb for at least 24 hours.

Preheat the oven to its lowest setting. Brown the lamb shoulder in a frying
pan in a little olive oil first, about 5 minutes on each side. Transfer to a
roasting pan and roast for 3½–4 hours. Halfway through the cooking time,
add the wine and water and cover with foil. The lamb is done when it comes
easily away from the bone. Remove all the meat from the bone, put it in a
serving dish and cover with foil. Keep it warm before serving, or chill and
reheat later. Reheating will take 45–60 minutes in the oven, at 140°C/fan
120°C/300°F/Gas 2.

The fennel and garlic sauce can be made up to 24 hours in advance. Preheat
the oven to 180°C/fan 160°C/350°F/Gas 4. Cut the fennel bulbs into thick slices
and brush with the oil. Bake for about 25–30 minutes, until softened and
browned in places. Add the garlic to the pan 10 minutes before the end of
the cooking time. Remove from the oven and allow to cool.

To serve the lamb:
flatbreads – allow plenty, e.g.
1 large lavash bread (30
× 40cm) per person, cut
into 20 × 20cm squares,
wrapped in clingfilm
to keep them soft until
needed

When the fennel bulbs and garlic have cooled completely, put in a food processor with all the other ingredients except the salt and mint leaves and process until you have a smooth sauce. Transfer to a serving dish, cover with clingfilm and chill until needed. Serve with the fresh mint leaves scattered over.

Serve all the elements of the main course together, placing the serving dishes in the centre of the table. Guests can help themselves to breads, add the lamb and fennel sauce, then wrap it up.

CIDER BABAS

Makes about 12 buns (the recipe can be doubled or quadrupled as needed; for 60, it will need to be made in batches)

Equipment: non-stick muffin or bun tray with 12 moulds, lightly greased with butter

Serving dish: large shallow bowl(s)

200ml cold milk
14g easy-bake dried yeast
300g plain flour
100g golden raisins
2 eggs plus 2 egg yolks
15g caster sugar
1 tsp salt
90g unsalted French butter, cold from the fridge, cut into 5mm cubes

For the syrup:
500ml West Country cider, or clear apple juice
600g caster sugar

To serve:
300ml crème fraîche or double cream

My search for an interesting pudding that could be prepared in advance ended with babas, sweet yeast buns steeped in syrup, which can be made up to 36 hours in advance. For our West Country-style babas, we made the syrup with local cider in place of traditional rum. This recipe is best made in an electric stand mixer, or it will be hard work mixing anything but small quantities.

Mix together the milk, yeast and ⅓ of the flour in the mixer bowl, then leave for 20 minutes until bubbling and active. Using the beater, not dough hook, beat in all the remaining ingredients, except the butter. Then, with the mixer on high speed, add the butter in batches.

Continue to beat the dough for 5 minutes. Remove the bowl from the mixer, take out the beater attachment and scrape it. Cover the bowl with clingfilm and leave to rise for 1–1½ hours in a warm, draught-free spot.

Preheat the oven to 180°C/fan 160°C/350°F/Gas 4. Beat the dough briefly with a wooden spoon to knock out the air. Using two tablespoons, one to scoop and the other to shape, spoon enough dough into each bun mould to fill it just over half full.

Leave the babas in a draught-free spot to rise. When they have doubled in size, bake for about 15 minutes until puffed, crisp and golden.

In the meantime, while the dough is rising, boil the cider and sugar together to make a syrup. Put the cooked babas in a container and pour over the syrup. Leave to soak, turning them once or twice. Serve the babas cold, with a bowl of cream on the table.

GARDEN PARTY

20 people

Our climate does not allow us to eat out on every summer's day, so when we can it is an event. These are often the most visual of feasts, all lit by sunshine with the table covered by a flapping cloth and on it a jam jar full of garden flowers. We linger over these meals lazily, putting all of the food, drink and all else that is needed on the table at once – so there are not too many trips to the kitchen.

These parties are a celebration of vegetable recipes and the garden, so varied in flavour, texture and colour few will notice the lack of meat or fish. The recipes are quite detailed, so suitable for a maximum of twenty people. The same dishes can of course be eaten as side dishes at a barbecue, or with a big roast like a whole pork loin, but a menu based only on vegetables and dairy solves the dilemma of what to cook when you expect an unknown number of vegetarian guests, or those whose diet excludes pork, red meat or shellfish. Another good purpose for the 'garden party' is that it can be very economical – a little frittata goes a long way. Serve plenty of bread plus butter or extra virgin olive oil for dipping.

ROAST BEETROOT

with fresh goat's curd cheese, honey and chilli

Serves: 20

Serving dish: large platter or shallow bowl

16 medium-sized raw beetroots, scrubbed very clean but not trimmed

6 tbsp olive oil, plus extra for the walnuts

3 tbsp balsamic vinegar

240g walnut halves

1kg fresh fresh goat's curd cheese, sliced

4–5 red chillies, deseeded and sliced

4 tbsp extra virgin olive oil

2 tbsp runny honey

4 tbsp parsley, chopped or micro leaves (optional)

salt and freshly ground black pepper

A very pretty salad to serve in any season. All the ingredients can be cut and prepared in advance, then assembled on plates 30 minutes before serving.

Preheat the oven to 190°C/fan 170°C/375°F/Gas 5. Place the beetroots whole in a roasting pan lined with foil and roll in the oil and vinegar. Cover with foil and roast for 45 minutes. Take off the foil and roast for another 15 minutes. Set aside to cool, then slice the beetroots – you may want to remove the skins but it is not necessary if the beetroots are clean.

Meanwhile, toast the walnuts in a little oil, over a low-medium heat. Be careful not to burn them. Tip out onto kitchen paper to remove excess oil then onto a board and roughly chop.

To assemble the salad: scatter the beetroot slices all over a large serving plate. Follow with the cheese slices, then the walnut pieces. Scatter the chillies over the top, then zigzag over the extra virgin olive oil and the honey. If using parsley or leaves, throw them over the surface. Season with salt and black pepper, then serve.

NEW POTATO AND WATERCRESS FRITTATA

Makes 1 frittata (serves 10, or 20 as part of the menu)

Serving dish: large board or flat plate

12 new potatoes, scrubbed

1 tbsp extra virgin olive oil

2 bunches watercress, tops only (no tough stalks)

salt and freshly ground black pepper

6 duck eggs, beaten with a pinch of salt

4 tbsp freshly grated Parmesan or pecorino cheese

The Italian answer to Spanish tortilla, frittata is not as thick in shape and is served dusted with grated fresh Parmesan or pecorino cheese. You can vary frittata to suit the season – see options opposite. You do not need to add potato to every frittata, but for the garden party it makes the frittata more substantial and filling. You will notice I make mine with duck eggs, not just because their yolks are a lovely colour but because they cling well to the vegetables. Hen's eggs are fine if duck eggs are not available.

Put the potatoes in a pan, cover with water and bring to the boil. Simmer for about 10 minutes until just tender. Drain, allow to cool, then cut into 5mm slices. Set to one side.

Preheat the grill to a medium-low setting. Heat the oil in a 20cm non-stick frying pan. Add the watercress and stir-fry for a minute or so until the leaves begin to wilt. Add the potatoes, season with a pinch of salt and a few grinds of black pepper, then stir to mix with the watercress.

Turn the heat right down and pour over the beaten egg. Cook very slowly. When the egg mixture has half-solidified and looks golden brown underneath if lifted with palette knife, place the pan under the grill to cook the surface. When the egg feels firm if pressed with a finger, remove from the heat.

Place a flat plate or board over the pan and invert it. When the frittata is cool, scatter the grated cheese generously over the surface.

SEASONAL FRITTATA

You adapt the suggestions below to the master recipe. Remember to dice or slice all but salad vegetables before adding the egg mixture. Using potato is optional.

Spring:

Purple sprouting broccoli
Asparagus
Rocket and new potato

Summer:

Garden pea and/or broad bean – with crisp pancetta
Courgette, with grated salted ricotta on top

Autumn:

Fungi – wild and cultivated mushrooms
Turnip and spinach

Winter:

Celeriac
Salsify
Potato and leek

SMOKY AUBERGINES

Serves: 10, or 20 as part of the menu

Serving dish: large shallow plate/serving dish

4 firm aubergines, not too large
1 tbsp salt
3 tbsp vegetable oil
2 tbsp chilli bean paste
2 tbsp soy sauce
4 tbsp Shaoxing rice wine
4 tbsp Chinese red vinegar
200ml vegetable stock
3 tbsp runny honey

To serve:
2 tbsp sesame seeds, toasted in a pan until golden
4 tbsp coriander leaves

A powerful, punchy-flavoured way to eat aubergines, with fermented chilli beans, soy and honey. The recipe is based on one in a favourite restaurant, A Wong, and very easy to make. It is important to make it with small, firm aubergines.

Cut the aubergines into long slices, 1cm thick. Put them in a colander, scatter over the salt, then toss to coat. Leave for 45 minutes then rinse and pat the aubergines dry.

You will have to cook the aubergines in two batches. Heat half the oil in a large pan and add half of the chilli bean paste. Fry for a few seconds then add half the soy sauce. Fry one half of the aubergine slices for 30 seconds on each side in this mixture then transfer to a plate. Repeat with the remaining aubergines in the remaining oil, chilli bean paste and soy sauce. Put all the fried aubergines in the pan and add the rice wine, vinegar, stock and honey and cook for a few minutes until soft.

Serve with the toasted sesame seeds and coriander leaves scattered over the surface.

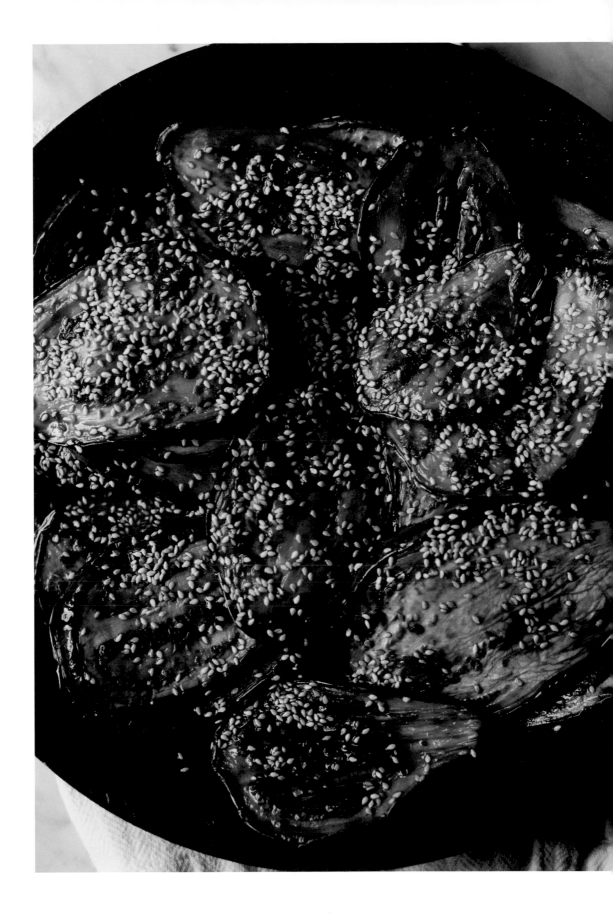

ROASTED RED PEPPERS
with egg mimosa

Serves: 10

Serving dish: large flat plate

olive oil, for brushing
5 red peppers, halved, seeds
   and stalk removed
5 eggs

To serve:
2 tbsp extra virgin olive oil
sea salt
3 tbsp flat-leaf parsley, leaves
   only, chopped

Soft, sweet, slightly burnt and blistered red peppers with the creaminess of finely grated egg yolk, another of my favourite vegetable dishes. There is one hard and fast rule that cannot be compromised: the peppers have to be roasted for long enough or they will be sour and disgusting. Green, orange or yellow peppers are unsuitable for this recipe.

Preheat the oven to 200°C/fan 180°C/400°F/Gas 6 and line two baking sheets with baking parchment. Brush the parchment with olive oil and then place the peppers, cut side down, on the baking sheets. Brush the surface lightly with oil.

Bake for about 20–30 minutes until the peppers are soft and the skin is blistered and dark in patches. Remove from the oven, place the peppers in a container with a lid or a plastic bag tied with a knot and allow them to steam while they cool.

Put the eggs in a pan and cover with water, then bring to the boil. Simmer for 8 minutes. Remove from the heat and place under the cold tap. When the eggs are cool, peel them and break open the white part to remove the whole firm yolks. Set these to one side. Chop the whites finely and set to one side.

When the peppers are cool, remove them from the container and peel off the skins. This is much easier to do if the peppers have been allowed to cool this way and are well enough cooked. Lay the peppers neatly side by side in one layer on a flat serving plate then zigzag over the extra virgin olive oil. Season with a pinch of sea salt then scatter over the chopped egg white.

Lastly, use a fine grater to grate the egg yolks over the surface of the peppers and egg whites – you will see why it is called eggs mimosa, like the yellow fuzzy flowering shrub. Throw over the parsley and serve.

COURGETTE AND FENNEL CRUSH

with crudités

Serves: 20

Serving dish: a large bowl or bowls

6 courgettes, pared and cut in half lengthways

2 fennel bulbs, sliced

4 garlic cloves, crushed

200ml extra virgin olive oil

5 tbsp tahini

juice of two lemons – or more

1 litre full-fat Greek yoghurt

sea salt and freshly ground black pepper

A fruity summer vegetable dip, enriched with creamy yoghurt and tahini. For dipping I like to choose vegetables other than the usual sticks of carrot, red pepper and celery. Whole radishes, bundles of summer leaves, strips of courgette or anything you can find that is young and sweet. For bulk you can also add halves of soft-boiled egg, boiled new potatoes or toasted flat breads.

Preheat the oven to 180°C/fan 160°C/350°F/Gas 4.

Place the courgette and fennel pieces on a baking tray with the garlic, brush generously all over with the olive oil (reserving a little for serving) then cover with foil. Bake for about 30 minutes until the vegetables are soft.

Place in a food processor with the tahini and lemon juice then chop until you have a rough mash. Transfer to a bowl, stir in the yoghurt then add seasoning to taste. Add a little more lemon if you feel the flavour needs sharpening. Transfer to a large bowl or individual serving bowls and then zigzag over the remaining olive oil.

INDOOR PICNIC

50–70 people

This is a format for an early evening
party, entertaining on quite a large
scale, on a low budget, without cooking
facilities. On three occasions I have
held a party at a venue with no place for
preparation, just a table in the middle
of the room, with no space for plates
and crockery. I had to serve 'hand food',
generous enough to fill the hungry with
their drinks. I wanted the food to look
good but could not afford canapés or
more than a few helpers.

Then I remembered the picnics of
my childhood, sometimes held in the
middle of a field, with just a car boot as
'table', and how we would make our own
sandwiches from a few good ingredients,
just in the palm of our hands. Ham and
smoked salmon, mustard, pickle and
bread. Taking this idea and making a
glorious table, the sugared ham being
the star in the middle, is something
I have done ever since and I always
recommend it to friends who have the
same dilemma. Typical sites include
community or village halls, barns,
commercial properties like shops or
warehouses, marquees or, of course,
your indoor picnic can always be
outdoors.

Over time I have added to the picnic.
Sometimes offering big bowls of potted
crab (see page 28) and curing my own
salmon – which is easy. When one of
my friends asked me to help with the
food for her own event, again on a tiny

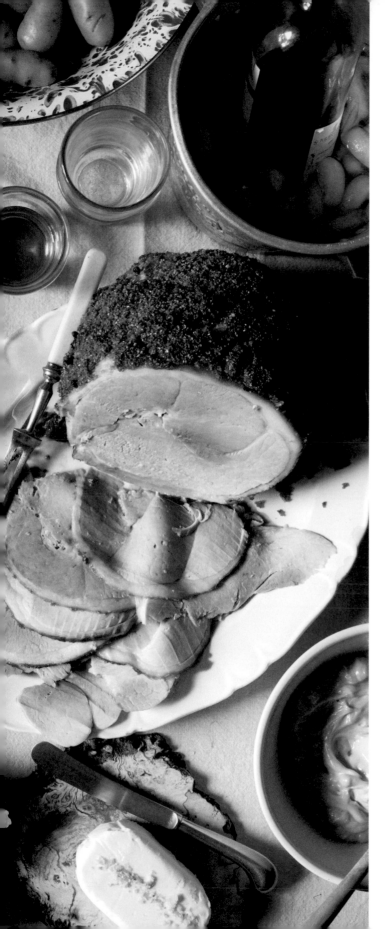

budget, for bulk we added a big wooden vegetable box of boiled small waxy Ratte potatoes and a bucket of homemade mayonnaise to the table. The party guests loved it. I have also put out plates of young root vegetables to dip in sauces such as the fennel and garlic sauce (see page 204).

Simplicity can be very stylish and, as always, if you use the best ingredients for your picnic, they will shine out; sources of raw gammon, salmon and bread can be found in the Directory (see pages 269–271). You can buy the ham ready-roasted from specialist suppliers, which can be excellent, though a ham that is still warm from being roasted and glazed that day is unbeatable.

For this party you will need someone to help you carve the ham and salmon.

The quantities below are for a stand-up drinks party with food for the hungry. I find some people eat a lot, but some very little – especially if they are eating later in the evening. Err on the side of generosity; leftover salmon and ham will not go to waste. If you are expecting many buy a very large ham, but make sure it will fit in your oven.

RAW ROOTS

To prepare beautiful raw vegetables for dipping, choose baby turnips, beetroot, carrots and also radishes. If the leaves are fresh and good-looking, keep them on. Wash them well, scrape off any hairy roots and ingrained dirt near the leaves. Place in a basket and cover with a damp cloth.

BREAD

Bread matters – it is a detail but an important one so, in good time before your party, decide on what you want and place an order to collect on the day. Serve artisan breads, white sourdough, spelt bread and rye with the salmon and ham. Have the loaves pre-sliced if possible, to save time. Serve good farmhouse butter. If you put out unsalted and salted, scatter a few sea salt crystals onto the salted butter so it can be identified. Put out several butter knives.

CHEESE

If you are uncertain about numbers, one or two whole cheeses will cover eventualities. Serve with pickles and buy extra bread. See Cheese party for advice (pages 176–179).

PICKLES AND CHUTNEYS

Choose a favourite chutney, the carrot pickle on page 32 or olive and fig pickle on page 178, or buy jars of good-quality readymade. Sources for these, plus good mustard, cornichons or other pickled vegetables can be found in the Directory, page 270.

POTATO BOX WITH MAYONNAISE

Serves: 50–70, as part of the suggested menu

Serving dish: wooden box for the potatoes; bowl for the mayonnaise

5kg Ratte potatoes, depending on number

For the mayonnaise (makes enough for 20):

12 egg yolks
3 tbsp Dijon mustard
1 litre groundnut, grapeseed or sunflower oil
juice of 1–1½ lemons
200ml extra virgin olive oil
¼ tsp ground white pepper
fine salt

A very humble nibble but always greeted enthusiastically by guests. Use Ratte potatoes, which are long and a bit knobbly, with golden-yellow flesh and a citrusy tang. They are native to northern France and often sold in a wooden tub, which I like to put them back into to serve. British Ratte or Anya potatoes are also suitable. The more common Charlotte potatoes can also be very good, or you might like a mix, including a few blue-fleshed potatoes. Pink Fir Apple potatoes are another option, but they go from undercooked to overcooked and falling apart in seconds so need careful watching.

Put the potatoes in a large pan and cover well with water. Add salt and bring slowly to the boil. Simmer for about 8 minutes but test the potatoes sooner – ideally they need to be still a bit sticky and waxy in the centre and floury on the outside. They will continue to cook for a minute after draining so remove from the heat as soon as you are satisfied they are done.

To make the mayonnaise, put the egg yolks and mustard in a large bowl. Whisk together then add the groundnut oil very slowly to begin with, whisking all the time. When a third of the groundnut oil has been incorporated, add it a little faster. Next, add the olive oil. When nearly all has been added, the sauce will be very thick. Add lemon juice to taste, then beat in the remaining oil including the olive oil. Finally, season with the white pepper and fine salt, to taste.

To serve the potatoes, line a wooden box, or basket or bowl, with a cloth and put the potatoes in whole. Put the mayonnaise in a bowl alongside, so guests can pick them up and dip straight into the sauce.

ROAST SUGARED HAM

Serves: 30, or 50–70 as part of the suggested menu

Serving dish: large platter, drip board or wooden board

1 whole gammon (about 6kg) or half-gammon (for a lower number)

2 tbsp ground coriander seeds

20 fennel seeds

12 juniper berries

1 tbsp ground black pepper

300ml black treacle

For the glaze:

60g English mustard powder

about 30 cloves

200g demerara sugar

To serve:

pickles of choice

English mustard and grainy Dijon mustard

chutney of choice

Buy your gammon (raw cured pork leg joint) on the bone, whether a half or whole, because otherwise they fall apart when the rind is removed after the first stage of the cooking. Pick it up two days in advance, because it will need to be soaked in water to remove some of the salt. You will be offered smoked or unsmoked (green). Choose smoked – the flavour will be subtle, less salty.

Put the gammon in the sink or a very large container and cover it with cold water. Leave to soak overnight.

Preheat the oven to 160°C/fan 140°C/325°F/Gas 3 and line a large roasting pan with two layers of foil. Place the ham in the pan. Mix the spices with the treacle and pour over the ham. Cover the ham by pinching the two sheets of foil together.

Bake the ham for approximately 3½–4½ hours, until a skewer inserted into the centre comes out easily and without too much resistance, indicating the meat inside is cooked. If using a meat thermometer, 60–62°C/140–144°F is perfect. Remove the ham from the oven, take off the foil cover and allow it to cool for about 15 minutes. Turn up the oven to 180°C/fan 160°C/350°F/Gas 4.

Lift the ham out of the pan, clean it and line it with baking parchment. Put the ham back into the pan. Using a small pointed knife, remove and discard the leathery rind from the ham, leaving the white fat intact.

Put the mustard powder in a bowl and add a small amount of water. Mix to a thick paste – it needs to be quite thick and dry for the sugar to stick. Stud the whole of the surface of the ham with cloves, about 2–3cm apart, then spread the mustard all over. Next, cover the ham with the demerara sugar – I find the best way to do this is to put sugar into my cupped hand and press it onto the surface of the fat. Put plenty of sugar on the ham.

Finally, bake the ham for 20 minutes, until the sugar has set into a golden crust. Remove the ham from the oven and allow to cool. It is juiciest served on the day. Serve with a selection of pickles, mustard and chutney.

WHISKY AND PEPPER-CURED SALMON

Makes 2 large sides of cured salmon. Serves 30, or 50–70 as part of the suggested menu

Serving dish: non-corrosive container or shallow dish, long enough to accommodate the salmon sides

2 × 1.5kg sides of fresh salmon, pin bones removed
200g soft brown sugar
200g salt
50g freshly ground black pepper
300ml whisky

To serve:
sliced fresh radishes
sliced cornichons

As an alternative to smoked salmon, the Scandinavian method of curing it with sugar and salt is one you can do yourself. It needs no cooking, no special equipment and the results are differently aromatic. You will need a very sharp knife to slice it thinly, which can be done an hour before serving with a sweet mustard, horseradish and turmeric sauce.

Put the salmon side skin down into the dish. Mix together the sugar, salt and pepper. Pour the whisky into the dish. Sprinkle the sugar mix onto the flesh of the salmon. Sandwich the second side onto it, skin side up. Cover the whole dish with two sheets of clingfilm and then place a board or piece of thick card cut to size on top of the fish. Put some weights onto the board to press the salmon down – cans of tomato or beans will do – and then place the container in the fridge for a minimum of 16 hours to cure, turning the salmon pieces over after 8 hours.

Discard the liquid that seeps out of the salmon. Pat the fish fillets dry with kitchen towels then wrap them in clingfilm until needed.

To slice the salmon, place a fillet skin side down. Beginning at the wider end, cut slices no more than 5mm thick, at a 25–30-degree angle. Serve with the radish and cornichon slices scattered over, and the sauce in a bowl beside it.

The salmon will keep for a week, if kept well wrapped in the fridge.

Option: For an alcohol-free cure, use 500g grated beetroot in place of the whisky and golden caster sugar instead of the brown sugar.

SUMMER LUNCH PARTY

8–12 people, seated

I love lazy summer lunch parties where the food is put on the table all together so no one needs to get up and fetch anything more than another bottle of something cool from the fridge. In warm weather appetites wane slightly, so serve lightweight dishes with plenty of fresh colourful vegetables. Dipping plates are perfect in these circumstances, with light and golden thin breads or crispy cos lettuce leaves for scooping. For the central dish in summer I love to serve either simple roast chickens, with homemade mayonnaise, or a baked fish or a heap of shellfish.

I first came across le grand aïoli, or Aïoli, when visiting my grandmother in France, and I still think of it as one of the greatest and most beautiful feasts to serve to a smaller number of people. Perfectly cooked cod, waxy new potatoes, crisp green salad and tomatoes, the season's first globe artichokes, soft-boiled eggs – all to be eaten with the garlic mayonnaise that gives the dish its name.

AÏOLI PLATTER

Serves: 8

Serving dish: large flat tray, platter or basket lined with fig or vine leaves

For the aïoli:

2–4 garlic cloves, or to taste

fine sea salt

6 egg yolks

200ml groundnut oil

100ml extra virgin olive oil

juice of 1 lemon

¼ tsp ground white pepper

For the platter:

8 free-range eggs

2kg medium–large new
potatoes, peeled

3–4 globe artichokes

2kg freshest cod loin

2 tbsp olive oil, plus extra
for the lemons

sea salt

4 lemons, halved

8 cos lettuce hearts, leaves
separated

3 tbsp whole Niçoise olives
or red-brown Ligurian
Taggiasca olives

For breath:

parsley sprigs

To serve:

good-quality bread

I do not make this recipe authentically with salt cod, because you need a really thick loin of best-quality saltfish, which is rarely available in the UK. Good fresh cod or good-quality frozen is absolutely suitable. Serve your feast with chilly rosé wine and plenty of bread on the table – you may be there for hours if there is enough aïoli. If you are nervous about serving a garlicky sauce like this to guests, simmer the peeled garlic in milk beforehand and offer small sprigs of parsley to guests to chew afterwards, which go a long way to remove the aftertaste.

To make the aïoli, slice the garlic then, using the side of a kitchen knife, crush it with a large pinch of salt until you have a wet paste. Put as much as you want into a large bowl with the egg yolks. Add a few drops of the groundnut oil and whisk. Slowly add both the oils, whisking all the time. The sauce will become very thick. Add a little lemon juice partway through to loosen the sauce. Continue until all the oil has been added then add more lemon juice to taste, and salt and white pepper to bring out the flavour. If you have been tasting the sauce, chew parsley before your guests arrive.

Prepare the platter ingredients. Put the eggs in cold water, bring to the boil and count 4½ minutes. Cool them in cold water, tap all over, then peel and cut in half. Boil the potatoes until they are just tender and waxy in the centre. Boil the artichokes for about 35–40 minutes until one of the lower leaves pulls away easily. Drain and cool.

Preheat the oven to 180°C/fan 160°C/350°F/Gas 4. Brush the cod loin with the oil and season with salt. Bake for about 10–14 minutes, until the flesh begins to flake. Remove from the oven. The flakes should be firm and a little translucent. Allow to sit at room temperature. Brush the lemon halves with oil and fry flesh side down until they colour and caramelise.

Place everything on one platter with the globe artichokes, potatoes, lettuce and eggs arranged all around the fish. Scatter the olives and lemons over the top. Put the aïoli in a bowl, have a large quantity of bread to hand, and feast.

CREAMED BUTTER BEANS

with flatbreads, fresh herbs, olives and feta

Serves: 6–8

**Serving dish: large
board or platter**

For the flatbreads:

150g Italian '00' pasta flour,
   sifted, plus extra for
   dusting

2 tbsp extra virgin olive oil,
   plus extra for brushing

½ tsp fine salt

80–120ml ice-cold water

sea salt and black sesame
   seeds (optional)

**For the butter
bean cream:**

2 × 450g cans butter beans

2 tbsp tahini (sesame paste)

3 garlic cloves, crushed

125ml Greek yoghurt

juice of 1 lemon, and more

sea salt

To serve:

fresh mint leaves, flat-leaf
   parsley, micro herbs and
   baby leaves (optional)

200g good quality 'barrel-
   aged' feta cheese,
   crumbled into pieces

black/green olives

extra virgin olive oil

freshly ground black pepper

A great low-price dish for a big dinner. The most humble of beans transform into silken cream with sesame paste, garlic and yoghurt. Presented in a pool, on a platter or board, with leaves and herbs, tart, crumbly feta and crisp flatbreads, the elegance of this will take you by surprise. If you do not want to make the breads, you can buy Sardinian crispbreads (pane carasau) made with olive oil.

To make the flatbreads, put the flour in a bowl and add the olive oil and salt. Add 80ml of the water and mix until you have a soft, smooth dough, adding more water if it does not come together. The dough should be slightly tacky but not really stick to your hands or the bowl. If it does, add a little more flour. Dust the dough ball lightly with flour, wrap in clingfilm and place in the fridge for 30 minutes.

Preheat the oven to 190°C/fan 170°C/375°F/Gas 5 and line a baking sheet with baking parchment.

Remove the dough from the fridge and cut into 8 pieces. By now it should not be tacky at all but soft and pliable. Dust the worktop with flour then roll one piece into a long strip. It will become tight and resist with too much rolling so stop for about 30 seconds to let the dough relax before rolling again. Make sure there is enough flour under the dough – and keep rolling until it is 20cm long and very thin, about 1mm. Repeat with the remaining pieces.

Lay the breads on the baking sheet, as many as will fit, and brush with olive oil. Sprinkle with salt and seeds (if using). Bake until pale gold and slightly puffed. Cool on a rack.

To prepare the creamed butter beans, place a colander or sieve over a bowl and strain the butter beans. Retain the liquid – some may be needed to loosen the texture of the cream. Put the butter beans, tahini, garlic, yoghurt and lemon in a food processor and blend until smooth.

Taste and season with salt; also add more lemon juice if you think it too rich. The texture should be soft like hummus – so add a little bit more of the butter bean liquid if it is too pasty. Adjust the seasoning again – it is really important that the cream is not bland.

Spread the cream onto a board or platter in ripples. Scatter over the herbs and leaves, feta and olives. Finally, zigzag over some extra virgin olive oil and sprinkle with black pepper. Serve as a sharing dish, with the flatbreads on the side.

Options: Replace the butter beans with frozen garden peas and a small handful of mint leaves, then dress with extra mint leaves. Alternatively, use very young broad beans or, if you don't mind a little extra work, the green centres of frozen broad beans. This is especially worthwhile, because they taste as good as fresh and cost very little.

CLAFOUTIS WITH PEARS

Serves: 6–8

Serving dish: ovenproof metal pan or ceramic dish.

30g butter, for greasing the pan

120g caster sugar, plus extra for dusting

100ml whole milk

150ml whipping cream

½ vanilla pod, seeds only, or ¼ tsp vanilla extract

4 eggs

20g plain flour

500g perfectly ripe pears, cut lengthways into eighths

The lightest baked creamy custard with soft fruit. I make clafoutis with pears, apricots, plums or figs but very rarely, although faithful to its origins, with cherries – because I am lazy about pitting (stoning) small fruit. Make the clafoutis an hour before serving. It only takes 20 minutes to prepare and can be made with slightly unripe fruit, which softens during cooking. You can also make it 'boozy', soaking the fruit in a tablespoon of corresponding liqueur – Poire Williams for the pears, plum brandy for plums and so on.

Preheat the oven to 190°C/fan 170°C/375°F/Gas 5. Butter the pan and then dust it with caster sugar. Put the milk, cream and vanilla in a saucepan and heat to boiling point then remove from the heat.

Put the eggs in a bowl with the sugar and whisk them together. Add the flour and whisk until smooth, then pour the milk mixture in slowly, whisking all the time.

Scatter the pears over the base of the pan – you can arrange them neatly in a circle if you wish. Pour the batter around them, not over the top, and then put the pan in the oven and bake for 20–25 minutes until the custard has puffed and coloured gold in places. Remove from the oven and allow to cool for 1 hour. Dust with caster sugar and serve.

TWO CHRISTMAS DINNERS

A feast to approach from a number of
angles, which tests the fortitude of any
cook or host – but really should not. In
fact, the real challenge is not to succumb
to doing too much, intimidated by the
season's ceaseless commercialism. I can
promise this: that if you do less, those
who enjoy your relaxed and stylish
Christmas food will think that you did
much more.

The following recipes are for two
different Christmas dinners, one
traditional and one that is best
described as grown-up. The traditional
Christmas, for a large number with
children included, is just that: virtually
Dickensian in its conventions, with a
goliath of a turkey, stuffing, gravy, bread
sauce, Brussels sprouts and then, of
course, a flaming plum pudding. This is
the Christmas of popping crackers and
fizz – it is also one that, with a solid plan,
will be as much fun for you as it is for
those excited children.

My other Christmas dinner is one for
a few people, those who are not woken
at six in the morning by hysterical
six-year-olds, and who take Christmas
Day slowly, with the ambition to drink
some very fine wine and avoid the toil
of getting a roast with all the trimmings
out of the oven. For them a simple roast
goose and a few elegant side vegetables
that can be prepared in no time. This
meal ends with little sweetmeats rather
than a flaming pudding, and, most
probably, cigars.

For an easy homemade Christmas, once you've shopped for the food and drink, all you need is a timetable. Be something of a field marshal about sticking to it, rope in the troops to help and, by Christmas morning when your home is a mayhem of relatives and other guests, matters should be in hand. Things do go wrong: technical trouble, the oven playing up; things that forgot to go on the shopping list; someone drinking the last of the cooking brandy; burnt parsnips (actually, that is a given) – there is no guarantee, except that it comes around the next year and you get to have another go. Laugh disasters off and look forward.

Needless to say, Christmas is more than one meal. If you have people to stay there is Christmas Eve dinner, possibly meals to think about for Boxing Day and even beyond. Unless you want to spend several days being a chef, can I suggest adopting the philosophy that everything after the main event is a vultures' picnic. On Christmas Eve, I roast a ham and glaze it with sugar (see page 222). We eat a part of it hot, with mashed potatoes. If anyone comes to stay, accept all offers of cheese, smoked salmon, terrines, pies, chutney, cakes, ice cream and chocolates. Buy a few ingredients to help transform leftovers: fresh herbs, limes, pastry and – whatever you do – have plenty of bread and potatoes about.

COUNTDOWN TO CHRISTMAS

ORDERING A TURKEY OR GOOSE

Order a turkey or goose online, or direct from a farm, butcher or supermarket, specifying the size – see below. I would not leave it to chance. 'Last order' dates are usually 10 days before Christmas Day. If you live near a producer, support them and buy local, if convenient.

Ideally, buy a traditional breed of turkey. There will be more moisturising fat under the skin, the meat has a wider grain and a stronger wild, gamey flavour – the brown leg meat is especially good. Choose either a Norfolk Bronze or Black-feathered turkey that has been reared outdoors, free range. For the crispest roasted skin, buy a bird that has been dry plucked, and, for depth of flavour, matured for a week non-eviscerated. These birds cost more, but the rewards are great. See the Directory on page 269. Farm suppliers who specialise in rearing geese outdoors for Christmas can also be found online.

TWO OR MORE DAYS BEFORE CHRISTMAS

- Make a supply of chicken stock
- Prepare the cranberry sauce
- Mix the brandy or rum butter
- If serving a ham, soak the gammon in cold water to remove excess salt

CHRISTMAS EVE

I like to have a free afternoon on Christmas Eve, turn on the radio carol service, and pour myself a glass of bubbly. Then, with list of tasks in front of me, the idea is to work through them one by one. When my children were small, I would ask my husband to take them out somewhere. These days they give me a hand – it gets easier. If you can complete the list before others arrive, it will make your Christmas Day a smoother ride.

- Make the pork and chestnut stuffing for the neck cavity
- Stuff the neck cavity of the bird, truss and secure the turkey and store it in a cool place
- Make the second fruit and pancetta stuffing; have it oven-ready, in a roasting pan
- Make the giblet stock, strain and refrigerate
- Prepare the seasoned milk for the bread sauce; make breadcrumbs and store them in a bag
- Peel the potatoes, cut in halves or quarters then leave in cold water

- Strip the outer leaves from the Brussels sprouts and trim the stalks
- Clean and trim any other vegetables, ready to cook
- Count and put to one side the crockery and cutlery, plus other tableware – you do not want to be hunting through cupboards for stuff on Christmas Day
- Choose serving platters and dishes, and set aside; fill salt cellars

CHRISTMAS DAY

The below is a guide to getting everything on the table at once, based on cooking a 5kg turkey serving 10–12 people. Use the timings opposite to bring the start time forward if cooking a larger turkey – so you have plenty.

3 HOURS BEFORE DINNER

Place a saucer in the base of the pan for steaming the pudding; fill with 5cm of water, put in the pudding – top open – and begin steaming. Depending on size, it will need 2½–3½ hours. It can be kept hot in the steamer. I have to add, even though a microwave-phobe, they are good for cooking puddings. Shop bought will have instructions on the packaging.

Preheat the oven/begin roasting the turkey. The turkey can be rested in a warm place for up to 1 hour after roasting – freeing up the oven space for potatoes etc.

2 HOURS BEFORE DINNER

- Parboil the potatoes, drain and allow to cool
- Strain seasoned milk for bread sauce; add breadcrumbs for soaking
- Baste the turkey twice during this period
- Warm the plates and serving dishes

1 HOUR BEFORE SERVING

- Remove ready turkey from pan, drain off the fat in the pan
- Place turkey on serving platter and wrap well with two sheets of foil, put it in a warm place to rest
- Make the gravy in the turkey pan, strain into a saucepan, ready to reheat
- Roast the potatoes
- Bake the second stuffing
- Bring water to boil for other vegetables
- Have ready some melted butter to dress other vegetables

30 MINUTES BEFORE SERVING

- Boil the Brussels sprouts, finish off in pan with chestnuts
- Reheat gravy and bread sauce
- Dress and finish other vegetables
- Transfer roast potatoes to warm serving dish, so they do not sit in fat
- Prepare to carve the turkey

TURKEY WEIGHTS AND COOKING TIMES

The cooking times below are based on stuffing the neck only and not wrapping the bird in foil. The oven temperature should be about 175°C, slightly less for a fan-assisted oven unless you can turn the fan off. When buying a whole turkey, allow approximately 450g per person.

3kg – serves 6–8   1¾ hours
5kg – serves 10–12   2¼ hours
7kg – serves 14–16   2¾ hours
9kg – serves 18–20   3½ hours
11kg – serves 22–26   4½ hours

TURKEY AND GOOSE

For a large number, and with enough oven space, serving a turkey and a goose together makes a very decadent dinner and also will please those who cannot stand goose.

SPECIAL DIETS

For guests who are vegetarian, there are main vegetable dishes worthy of a feast on pages 102–128. One Christmas when we invited a guest who could not eat pork, we replaced the sausage meat in the neck stuffing with minced duck breast. It was costly, but very good. You can buy duck sausages online but check that they are pure duck. In the same circumstances, omit the pancetta from the second stuffing.

CHRISTMAS TURKEY

with two stuffings and all the trimmings

Serves: 10–12

Serving dish: large platter

5kg turkey

I do not stuff the main cavity of the turkey because the turkey will be overcooked in an effort to make sure the stuffing is cooked through. I do stuff the neck cavity which is under the oven-ready bird. The second stuffing is cooked in a separate dish.

PORK SAUSAGE AND CHESTNUT STUFFING

– for the neck cavity

1 turkey liver and heart, finely chopped (optional)

500g pork sausage meat

50g pitted prunes, finely chopped

250g chestnuts, cooked and peeled, roughly chopped

small pinch of ground cloves

1 tbsp brandy

Combine all the ingredients in a bowl then spoon the stuffing into the neck cavity, which is at the base of an oven-ready bird. Put as much stuffing as you can inside the cavity, making sure that the skin flap that covers the cavity can be drawn across it and secured in place by two skewers.

The stuffing should be sealed inside so it does not leak out during cooking. If you have stuffing left over, form it into rounds the size of golf balls and bake for 30 minutes alongside the turkey.

APPLE, SAGE, PANCETTA AND PRUNE STUFFING
— *to roast separately*

4 tbsp pine nuts

3 tbsp butter or duck fat

300g white sourdough bread, torn into small pieces

8 sprigs thyme, leaves only

10 sage leaves, chopped

8 rashers pancetta, cut into small pieces

4 eating apples, cored and finely chopped

150g dried soft figs, roughly chopped

4 onions, finely chopped

4 celery sticks, finely chopped

3 eggs, beaten

sea salt and freshly ground black pepper

Put the pine nuts in a dry pan and toast over a medium-low heat until golden. Remove from the pan and set to one side.

Add half the fat to the pan and fry the bread until golden, then drain on kitchen paper and set to one side. Add the remaining fat, plus the herbs, pancetta, apples, figs, onions and celery, then stir-fry for a while, until the pan contents are warmed through. Remove from the heat, transfer to a bowl and allow to cool.

Add the bread and pine nuts to the bowl with the beaten egg. Season well and then mix thoroughly. Butter an ovenproof dish and then add all the stuffing mixture.

Bake at 175°C (same oven as the turkey if space) for 30–40 minutes until cooked through and golden on the surface. Cover with foil and store in a warm place until you serve.

GIBLET STOCK
— *to use in gravy*

2 tbsp vegetable oil

turkey giblets, excluding liver

1 onion, chopped

1 celery stick, sliced

1 carrot, sliced

1 bay leaf

1 sprig thyme

5 peppercorns

3 juniper berries, crushed with the side of a knife

1.5 litres water

salt, to taste

Heat the oil in a large pan, add the giblets and briefly brown all over. Add the vegetables and spices, fry for about 3 minutes then add the water. Bring up to simmering point, then allow to simmer for 1 hour. Taste and season with salt, then strain through a sieve, reserving the liquid. Store the giblet stock in the fridge.

ROASTING THE TURKEY

Equipment: large roasting pan, extra-wide aluminium foil, baking parchment and string

4 tbsp butter or duck fat, melted

For the main cavity:

2 strips pared lemon zest
1 bunch rosemary
1 bunch thyme
1 bunch sage
1 onion, halved
2 tbsp butter

Use the lemon zest to tie all the herbs together in a bunch. Place the onion and butter inside the turkey's main cavity, then put the bouquet of herbs in the mouth of the main cavity. Truss the turkey legs close together at the foot end, bringing them together one crossed over the other. Tie tightly with string.

Brush the whole turkey with some of the melted butter or duck fat. Put the remaining fat in the base of the pan. Cover the neck cavity and the feet end of the turkey drumsticks with a protective layer of foil or baking parchment covered with foil. This will prevent them burning and giving the juices that run from the bird a bitter taste.

Preheat the oven to 180°C/fan 160°C/350°F/Gas 4. A 5kg turkey with stuffing in the neck cavity takes 2¼ hours to roast. Baste the turkey twice during cooking. Ovens vary – place a strip of foil lightly over the surface of the turkey if you feel the breast skin is becoming too brown. (See cooking times guide, page 237.)

When the cooking time is up, test the turkey to see if it is done. Insert a long skewer into the deepest part of the thigh, through into the breast meat. Push a tablespoon against the skin and the point of the skewer's entry, and allow the juices to flow into it. If the juices are clear the meat is done; if they are pink, return the turkey to the oven and cook for another 15 minutes before testing again.

When the meat is done, lift the turkey from the roasting pan (in which the gravy is to be made) and place on a platter. Cover the turkey with two layers of wide foil and leave to rest (for up to 1 hour).

To carve the turkey, cut slices of the white meat from the breast vertically, across the grain. Remove the legs one at a time and carve the brown meat from them. Serve each person with brown and white meat, plus stuffing from the neck cavity and the second stuffing.

GRAVY

2 tbsp white wine,
   vermouth, marsala or
   sherry (optional)
1.3 litres giblet stock
salt, to taste

Tip the dripping from the roasting pan into a bowl, leaving behind juices
and any sweet matter that is stuck to the pan. Place the pan over a medium
heat; when it sizzles add the wine or other liquor and scrape the pan with a
wooden spoon to deglaze the sweet bits from the base. You can do this with
a little of the stock only if you wish. Add the (remaining) stock, bring to the
boil and simmer for a minute or two. Taste for salt – you will not need it if the
stock is seasoned – then pass the gravy through a sieve and keep warm in a
saucepan over a low heat until needed.

For thick gravy, add 1 heaped tablespoon of plain white flour to the pan with a
tablespoon of dripping. Mix to a paste over a low heat then add the wine and/
or stock in stages, stirring all the time. Pass through a sieve and store as above,
before serving.

CRANBERRY SAUCE

Boil 300g cranberries with 2 tablespoons of port or red wine. Add a little
maple syrup or light brown sugar to taste if desired.

BREAD SAUCE

Makes 1 litre

2 onions, halved
8 cloves
4 peppercorns
a few gratings of nutmeg
750ml whole milk
300g fresh white
   breadcrumbs, or more
3 tbsp butter
150ml cream
salt, to taste

Stud the onion halves with the cloves. Place in a pan with the spices and
milk and bring to the boil. Turn off the heat and leave the milk to absorb the
flavours for a minimum of 30 minutes, then strain the liquid through a sieve
and return it to the pan.

Reheat the milk 15 minutes before serving, adding enough breadcrumbs with
the butter and cream to make a thick, sloppy sauce. Season to taste with salt.
If the sauce is too stodgy, add a little fresh milk – it should be creamy and
runny.

BRUSSELS SPROUTS AND CHESTNUTS

1.5–2kg Brussels sprouts, stalks trimmed, outer leaves removed

2 tbsp olive oil

1 sprig rosemary, leaves only, chopped

200g peeled cooked chestnuts, quartered

Rosemary is a good counter to any sulphurous flavour in sprouts, though today's sprout breeds are sweeter.

Bring a pan of water to the boil, add the sprouts and cook until just tender. Drain, refresh under the cold tap to set the colour, and set aside. Do not store sprouts after cooking for more than 10 minutes or they can spoil.

Meanwhile, put the oil, rosemary and chestnuts in a pan and fry gently over a medium heat. Add the sprouts to warm through. Transfer all to a serving dish and keep warm until serving.

FAIL-SAFE ROAST POTATOES AND OTHER VEGETABLES
– see pages 118 and 122–125

CHRISTMAS PUDDING
and brandy butter

Serves 10–12

Serving dish: shallow dish

2kg Christmas pudding –
  follow maker's cooking
  times
3 tbsp cognac or rum,
  to serve

For the brandy butter:
250g softened unsalted
  French butter (less likely
  to curdle)
200g caster sugar
1 tsp orange zest (optional)
50–70ml cognac or dark
  rum

Beat the butter until pale and fluffy. Add the caster sugar and beat until the mixture is nearly smooth – the sugar crystals melt as they are beaten. Stir in the orange zest (if using). Chill the mixture for 10 minutes to stabilise it. Very carefully fold in the cognac or rum – if the mixture is too warm the alcohol will curdle it. Transfer to the serving bowl and chill.

To steam the pudding, you will need a pan with a well-fitting lid that accommodates the pudding in its basin.

Place a saucer in the base of the pan. Add 5cm of water and the pudding, cover with the lid and steam for the time recommended by the manufacturer – you can also use a microwave to cook a pudding, following timings on the packaging. When ready to serve, remove from the steaming pan, invert onto a shallow serving dish and take to the table. Be careful if flaming the pudding. Heat the cognac or rum in a small saucepan but do not let it boil. Have ready a long match. Pour the hot liquor over the pudding and then flame it with a lit match. When the flames die, slice and serve the pudding, with the brandy butter on the side.

ROAST GOOSE
with baked apples

Serves: 8 generously

Equipment: string, large-size aluminium foil and two large roasting pans

6kg goose
salt and freshly ground
 black pepper
1 garlic bulb
5 bay leaves

For the baked apples:
10 dessert apples (Cox's
 or Russets)
3 tbsp melted butter
2 tsp thyme leaves

For the gravy
goose giblets
1 litre chicken stock or
 water, or a mixture of
 the two if you do not
 have enough stock
1 onion, sliced
1 celery stick, sliced
1 carrot, peeled and sliced
1 bay leaf
1 sprig thyme
1 sprig parsley

A scaled-down dinner for food and wine lovers, and friends, when you want to celebrate Christmas but not in total traditional style. A goose is a wonderful piece of meat, perhaps the ultimate, especially after slow cooking. The skin, dark and crisp, is possibly one of the most delicious things I have ever eaten. The side dishes for this menu are simple, the idea being that this is a lazier meal to be made and enjoyed at leisure. Do order a goose that is a little larger than you will need but be aware that they must be able to fit in your oven. Serve with apple jelly, which can be made days, if not weeks, in advance – see recipe opposite. You can also use bought readymade apple jelly.

TO ROAST THE GOOSE:

Preheat the oven to 160°C/fan 140°C/325°F/Gas 3. Cut one sheet of aluminium foil and place in one of the roasting pans. Boil a kettle. Put the goose in the sink, pour boiling water over it – the whole kettleful – and pat dry; this will help crisp the skin.

Season the bird inside and out with salt and pepper. Place the whole garlic bulb in the cavity, with the bay leaves. Truss the goose with the string, tying the legs close to the body. This will help keep the breast juicy as the legs cook.

Use a skewer to prick the fatty parts of the bird all over, including the 'parson's nose', to help release the fat during cooking.

Place in the foil-lined pan and roast for 1½ hours. Remove from the oven. A lot of fat will have run from the bird into the base of the pan. Place the second pan close beside the first. Use two carving forks to lift the bird out of the first pan and into the second. Wrap the legs in foil, twisting it around the drumsticks to prevent burning.

Allow the fat in the first pan to cool a little, pour it into a heatproof container and store. Clean the pan and prepare it for the roast potatoes (see page 118).

Put the goose back into the oven and roast for a further 1–1½ hours, basting regularly.

The goose is done if the juices in the thigh meat run clear when the leg is pierced with a skewer and the meat tenderly comes away from the bone. Depending on your oven, you may need to give it 15–30 minutes longer.

Place the goose on a serving dish and cover loosely with two sheets of foil – so the skin stays crisp. Put in a warm place to rest for 20 minutes before serving.

To carve the goose, cut long oval slices across the grain from the fattest part of the breast meat, working your way towards the breastbone. Ensure that everyone is served the crisp skin.

Note: Cooking times for smaller geese are shorter: a 4kg goose will need 1–1½ hours, a 5kg goose a total of 2–2½ hours – but do test the colour of the juices.

TO PREPARE THE APPLES:

About 45 minutes before the goose is cooked, cut the apples in half across the core. Brush them with the melted butter then put them, cut side up, in an ovenproof dish. Bake them for about 20 minutes in the same oven as the goose, until the apples are soft and slightly collapsed. Remove and keep them in a warm place until needed.

FOR THE GRAVY:

While the goose is roasting in the first pan (or in advance the day before) put the giblets in a large pan, cover with the chicken stock and bring to the boil. Simmer for 45 minutes, strain and reserve.

Tip the cooled fat from the second roasting pan into the giblet pan, place it over a medium heat and add a glass of sherry or wine. Allow to simmer for a minute, then pour in the giblet stock. Bring to the boil and simmer for about 10 minutes. Skim off any fat and pour into a gravy jug or small pan. Keep it hot.

APPLE JELLY

(make several days in advance)

15 apples (windfalls are
ideal), quartered but not
cored
preserving sugar
2 sprigs thyme

Put the fruit in a large, heavy-based pan and add about 600ml of water. Cook, uncovered, over a very low heat for about 45 minutes, to a soft pulp.

Line a colander with muslin and set it over a dish, or set up a hanging jelly bag. Spoon the apply pulp into the bag and leave to drip through, but do not push the juice through or you will end up with cloudy jelly.

Measure the juice that has dripped through the cloth. Put it in a large pan and for each 500ml juice add 1kg preserving sugar. Bring to the boil and simmer for about 15 minutes, until it reaches setting point. To test this, drizzle a spoonful of jelly onto a cold plate and leave for a couple of minutes; a skin should form on top.

Pour into clean jam jars, add a sprig of thyme to each, seal and store. You can use the jelly within 24 hours of making, or it can be stored for about 3 months.

WATERCRESS, ORANGE AND FRESH FIG SALAD

4 oranges
6 ripe figs
4 bunches watercress,
leaves only
Handful of walnuts, broken
into pieces
3 tbsp walnut or hazelnut oil
or extra virgin olive oil
sea salt and freshly ground
black pepper

Lovely and fresh with the goose – and gorgeously pretty, especially if you can find blood oranges.

Pare the rind from the oranges, leaving just the flesh exposed – no pith. Cut out the segments – again, flesh only – leaving the membrane and centre of the orange behind.

Quarter the figs. Put the watercress on a plate and scatter the fruit and nuts over. Zigzag over the oil and then season with the salt and pepper.

BAKED SLICED POTATOES

(see page 119)

THREE LITTLE SWEETS

As nice to give away as they are to nibble. Chocolate truffles, obviously one of the most decadent sweets, are an obvious choice to make but I urge you to make the two others. They may seem more worthy but both have a beautiful flavour – the kirsch in the raw truffles tastes as naughty as chocolate.

1. RAW DATE AND HONEY TRUFFLES

Makes 30

250g dates
125g macadamia nuts
2 tsp cocoa
½ tsp coffee extract
2 tsp honey
2 tbsp kirsch
4 tbsp pine nuts and chopped, unsalted pistachio nuts

Put the dates, nuts, cocoa, coffee, honey and kirsch in a food processor and blend until you have a smooth-ish texture. Toast the pine nuts in a dry pan, until golden, then allow to cool. Make balls of the truffle mixture then roll in either the pine nuts or pistachio nibs.

2. CHOCOLATE TRUFFLES

Makes 40 small truffles

135g double cream
225g chocolate nibs or finely chopped chocolate (minimum 70% cocoa solids)
60g butter
4 tbsp good-quality cocoa powder, for dusting, on a plate

Put the cream in a pan and warm it over a low heat. Before it boils, add the chocolate. Allow the mixture to stand for 10–12 minutes without stirring then mix well. If there are still lumps of chocolate, warm again over a very low heat and stir until completely smooth. Cool for about 15 minutes in the fridge, until the mixture is like softened butter. Use two teaspoons to roll into lozenges then roll these in cocoa powder. Store the truffles in a cool place – not the fridge.

3. APRICOT AND PECAN MACAROONS

Makes 60

4 egg whites
270g icing sugar
80g soft dates, finely chopped
80g soft dried apricots, finely chopped
100g pecans, finely chopped

Preheat the oven to 160°C/fan 140°C/325°F/Gas 3. Whisk the egg whites with the icing sugar for approximately 10 minutes until stiff then carefully fold in the dried fruit and nuts. Pipe little heaps on a baking sheet lined with baking parchment. Bake for 15 minutes until risen a little and crisp. Remove from the sheet with a palette knife – you will need to make in batches.

MAKING A MENU
Matching courses – balancing a meal by season, look and flavour

It takes a little practice and comes more naturally to some than others but there is a useful system for making a good menu. I have mentioned before that choosing what others would like to eat is about sensitivity: a balance of the right foods, for the right day, suitable for your chosen group of guests. It is essentially the reverse of choosing off a menu in a restaurant – you are the menu and your guests the customer, as it were – put yourself in their shoes. To make this a little clearer, I have added notes based on season, flavour and colour to every recipe (see pages 256–261). You do not have to follow any rules exactly, but try to balance dishes. I try to visualise the dishes beside each other – even though they may be served as separate courses – and I ask the following three questions, in no order of importance:

SEASON

Eating food in season always works. Is it spring/summer or autumn/winter? You do not have to be more specific than this, although you can if you want. Climate is a thought – if it is a wet and chilly summer, a warming dish, which contains a seasonal food, will go down well and please everyone. On an unseasonably warm day in February, a zesty springtime course will fit the mood. Note also that some recipes suit all seasons.

LOOK

It may seem absurd but a menu can lose balance if everything is the same colour. Greens in the starter and main followed by a lime pudding, for example, feels one-directional. It is easy to avoid repeating colour, though it is fine to have a red starter, like tomatoes and a red pudding, like strawberries, if there is something contrasting in between. Texture is also important – a soup is not good before a main dish that has a lot of liquid; two courses that are fried should not be side by side. These disciplines quickly become common sense.

FLAVOUR

If the flavour of the first course contrasts with the second, you are on the right track. Some classify flavour into three groups, best defined as delicate, mellow and full, then balance their menu with, say, a light-flavoured starter followed by a more powerfully flavoured main course. I think this is not easy, and not quite enough. Recipes with their combination of ingredients create more detail and merit a little more description, so below I have made a note beside each recipe in the book that should tell you its overall 'effect'. All you have to do is balance the effect of each meal. This can mean contrast, so a 'cool' starter, followed by a 'robust' main course and a 'zesty' pudding. Alternatively the weather might dictate all courses to be 'warming' or, supposing your guests are not big eaters, you might want to combine recipes with a 'raw' or 'sprightly' effect.

I have also made some menu suggestions on pages 262–265.

RECIPE EFFECTS

Cool	Muscular	Smoky
Earthy	Piquant	Spicy
Elegant	Powerful	Sprightly
Exotic	Punchy	Warming
Fresh	Rich	Zesty
Gentle	Robust	
Mellow	Salty	

FIRST COURSES:
Meat and Fish

Ham, cider and watercress terrine
with mustard mayonnaise and
carrot pickle
Piquant – All seasons

Pork, duck and pistachio terrine
Rich – All seasons

Fishcakes with lemongrass and
coriander
Zesty – All seasons

White fish and avocado carpaccio
Clean – Spring/Summer

Fennel and apple carpaccio with
toasted walnut pesto
Sprightly – Spring/Summer

Beef carpaccio with red leaves and
ewe's milk cheese
Muscular – Summer/Autumn/
Winter

Roast bone marrows with parsley-
caper relish and toast
Rich – Autumn/Winter

Potted crab with Melba toast
Robust – Summer/Autumn

Little Lyonnaise salad
Punchy – Spring/Summer/Autumn

Char ceviche with lime, sesame
and fresh wasabi
Exotic – Spring/Summer

Whisky and pepper-cured salmon
Piquant – Autumn/Winter/Spring

FIRST COURSES: *Vegetable and Dairy*

Asparagus with hollandaise
Gentle – Spring

Rice-paper garden rolls with cucumber, watercress and avocado, with honey and lime sauce
Clean – Spring/Summer

Tomato and mustard tart
Powerful – Summer/Autumn

Baked whole cheese with toast spoons and chicory
Warming – Autumn/Winter

Poached egg and herb tartlets with caper and lemon dressing
Elegant – Spring/Summer

Roast beetroot with goat's curd cheese, honey and chilli
Sprightly – Spring/Summer

Smoky aubergines
Powerful – Autumn/Winter

Roasted red peppers with egg mimosa
Mellow – Spring/Summer

Creamed butter beans with flatbreads and fresh herbs, olives and feta
Earthy – All seasons

FIRST COURSES: *Soups*

Watercress velvet soup over sautéed black pudding, potato and bacon
Muscular – Autumn/Spring

Creamed squash and apple soup, with porcini buttered toasts and chestnuts
Robust – Autumn/Winter

Tomato soup over toasted cheese sandwiches
Comforting – Summer/Autumn

Beef bone marrow and beetroot soup over new potatoes
Powerful – Autumn/Winter

Chicken broth with spring vegetables and pistou sauce
Zesty – Spring/Summer/Autumn

MAIN COURSES:
Meat and Fish

Classic fish pie
Warming – All seasons

Rare roast sirloin of beef with Béarnaise sauce
Muscular – Autumn/Winter

Rare roast sirloin of beef with horseradish, rocket and radish salsa
Powerful – Spring/Summer

Rare roast sirloin of beef with lime, fried mint and chilli salsa
Exotic – Summer/Autumn/Winter

Rare roast sirloin of beef with lemon and espelette pepper butter
Piquant - Summer/Autumn

Rare roast sirloin of beef 'tagliata'
Robust – Summer/Autumn

Roast sugared ham
Robust – Autumn/Winter

Pork and cockles with samphire and lettuce
Salty – Autumn/Winter

Simple baked whole brill with beurre blanc
Graceful – Spring/Summer/Autumn

Poached arctic char with soy, ginger and spring onions
Salty – Spring/Summer

Poached salmon with hollandaise
Rich – Summer

Coq au vin
Warming – Autumn/Winter

Pigeon breasts with figs and parsley pearl barley
Powerful – Summer/Autumn

Guinea fowl, chicken and leek pie
Warming – Autumn/Winter/Spring

Cassoulet
Robust – Autumn/Winter

Aïoli feast with baked cod, potatoes, eggs and roast lemon
Punchy – Spring/Summer

Kitchari
Spicy – All seasons

Coconut chilli chicken
Powerful – All seasons

Marinated slow-cooked lamb shoulder with roast fennel, garlic sauce and flatbreads
Punchy – Spring/Summer

Slow-roasted duck legs with spiced barley
Warming – All seasons

MAIN COURSES:
Pasta, Rice and Vegetable

Game ragù with pasta
Robust – Summer/Autumn/Winter

*Baked penne with chopped beef,
pancetta and chicken livers*
Robust – Autumn/Winter

*Lemon risotto with rocket and
rocket flowers*
Zesty – Spring/Summer

New potato and watercress frittata
Sprightly – Spring/Summer

*Vegetable biryani with coconut
baked under a crust*
Powerful – All seasons

*Roast squash puff pastry pie with
watercress and fresh goat's curd*
Warming – Autumn/Winter

*Roasted mushrooms on sourdough
toast with a red wine sauce*
Earthy – Autumn/Winter

*Crispy potato cakes with garden
pea and lettuce sauce*
Robust – Spring/Summer

Broad bean and pea toasts
Elegant – Spring/Summer

SIDES

*Baked sliced potatoes with stock
and garlic*
Spring/Summer

Fail-safe roast potatoes
All seasons

Pommes purée
All seasons

Braised lentils
All seasons

Macaroni cheese
Autumn/Winter

Kale with apple and walnuts
Autumn/Winter

*Greens with lemon and rosemary
butter*
Spring/Summer

*Flageolet beans and cavolo nero
purée*
Spring/Summer

Tomato salad
Summer/Autumn

PUDDINGS

Chocolate mousse
Rich – All seasons

Iced chocolate parfait
Cool – All seasons

Caramelised oranges with salt
Mellow – Autumn/Winter

Crème caramel
Elegant – All seasons

Clafoutis with pears
Warming – Autumn/Winter

Apple crumble
Robust – Autumn/Winter

Tarte aux Pommes
Gentle – All seasons

Berry trifle
Sprightly – Spring/Summer

Chou chou pudding
Punchy – All seasons

Limoncello crêpes
Zesty – Spring/Summer

*Raspberry angel food cake with
raspberry jam and cream*
Elegant – Summer/Autumn

Pink grapefruit sorbet
Cool – All seasons

Cider Babas
Rich – Autumn/Winter

SAMPLE MENUS

The following sample menus include recipes from the 'Party' section, so do remember to scale down serving size accordingly.

Potted crab with Melba toast

Rare roast sirloin of beef with béarnaise sauce

Apple crumble

Pork, duck and pistachio terrine

Pigeon breasts with figs and parsley pearl barley

Pink grapefruit sorbet

Fennel and apple carpaccio with toasted walnut pesto

Poached salmon with hollandaise

Crème caramel

Creamed squash and apple soup

Cassoulet

Cider babas

Little Lyonnaise salad

Guinea fowl, chicken and leek pie

Cheese

Poached egg and herb tartlets

Rare roast sirloin of beef with lemon and Esplette pepper butter

Raspberry angel food cake

Whisky and pepper-cured salmon

Coq au vin

Clafoutis with Pears

White fish and avocado carpaccio

Slow-roasted duck legs with spiced barley

Limoncello crepes

Beef bone marrow and beetroot soup

Roast sugared ham

Chou chou pudding

Potted crab with Melba toast

Pork and cockles with samphire and lettuce

Limoncello crepes

Asparagus with hollandaise

Rare roast sirloin of beef with horseradish, rocket and radish salsa

Apricot and pecan macaroons

Creamed squash and apple soup

Marinated slow-cooked lamb shoulder

Caramelised oranges

Ham hock terrine

Classic fish pie

Cheese

Watercress velvet soup

Cassoulet

Crème caramel

Fish cakes with lemongrass and coriander

Rare roast sirloin of beef with lime, fried mint and chilli salsa

Pink grapefruit sorbet

Courgette tart

Rare roast sirloin of beef 'tagliata'

Raspberry angel food cake

Tomato and mustard tart

Rare rost sirloin of beef with béarnaise sauce

Berry trifle

Asparagus with hollandaise

Simple baked whole brill with beurre blanc

Chou chou pudding

Rice-paper garden rolls

Poached Arctic char with soy, ginger and spring onions

Iced chocolate parfait

Beef carpaccio with red leaves and ewe's milk cheese

Poached salmon with hollandaise

Tarte aux pommes

Roast bone marrows with parsley-caper relish and toast

Slow-roasted duck legs with spiced barley

Chocolate mousse

Chicken broth

Baked penne

Caramelised oranges

Whisky and pepper-cured salmon

Pork and cockles with samphire and lettuce

Apricot and pecan macaroons

Buffalo mozzarella rolls

Game ragù with egg pasta

Pink grapefruit sorbet

SAMPLE MEAT-FREE MENUS

Creamed butter beans with flatbreads and fresh herbs, olives and feta

Roasted mushrooms on sourdough toast with a red wine sauce

Chou chou pudding

———————

Fennel and apple carpaccio with toasted walnut pesto

Lemon risotto with rocket and rocket flowers

Tarte aux pommes

———————

Smoky aubergines

Vegetable biryani

Berry trifle

———————

Tomato soup over toasted cheese sandwiches

New potato and watercress frittata

Clafoutis with pears

———————

Roast beetroot with goat's curd, honey and chilli

Crispy potato cakes with garden pea and lettuce soup

Caramelised oranges

———————

Roast red peppers with egg mimosa

Roast squash puff pastry pie

Chocolate mousse

DRINK

What to drink with the food you give others is the subject of experts and I heartily recommend the books opposite. If you find your interest growing, especially with wine, you can fill many enjoyable hours engaged in that pursuit and also bookshelves with books containing a vast body of advice and knowledge. A trusted wine merchant will also make suggestions, though beware vested interest and rely on those who recommend across the price spectrum.

If I, as a cook, can offer any advice, however, it is to beware snobbery and to keep in mind that well-matched wine and food must complement each other. It is a huge treat to be given a rare and special wine with dinner, but it should not intimidate the occasion or the food. Equally it is wonderful for a well-made, modest wine to be served with food – in fact this is often the most stylish pairing of all. Knowing where to find such wines, and how best to use them, is a journey that feels rather winding and precarious at first, then becomes simpler as you find wines that work easily.

This journey ended for me with two affordable* wines – and that was twenty years ago and we still open bottles of both at most but not all dinners and parties. No one has ever called us dull (to our faces), but my favourite white with food is Tariquet chardonnay from the Gascony vineyards that are also home to the makers of Armagnac. The red in our home is a Bordeaux – a claret – Chateau Vircoulon. Both are so balanced you do not notice except to think, afterwards, that the wine and food danced without missing a step. But whilst I am married to these two, I have had brief love affairs with all sorts of wine, from all over, while occasionally being lucky enough to sample some at deity level.

Beer, cider and other drinks have their places with food – though for me none share the complex and forensic interest in matching the cultures of food and wine.

*£10 or just under (2017)

A small collection of books on drink (with food)

Malcolm Gluck and Mark Hix, *The Simple Art of Marrying Food and Wine* (Mitchell Beazley, 2005)

Andrew Jefford, *Choosing Wine* (Ryland Peters & Small, 2003)

Hugh Johnson, *Pocket Wine Book* (Mitchell Beazley, 2017)

Victoria Moore, *How to Drink* (Granta Books, 2010)

Jancis Robinson, *24-Hour Wine Expert* (Harry N Abrams, 2016) – see also www.jancis robinson.com

SUPPLIER DIRECTORY

A list of reliable sources. You will have your own favourite local shops which I very much encourage you to use, but you will find in this list retailers of rare ingredients plus trusted suppliers of certain specialist foods, most of which deliver. Kitchen equipment and party-hire firms are at the base of the list.

GROCERS

Waitrose www.waitrose.com
Good for: a very wide variety of ingredients, including confit duck, brown shrimps, buffalo ricotta, bone marrow, unsalted pistachios, butter pastry (Dorset Pastry Co.), sourdough bread, game birds, baking ingredients, world foods and fresh herbs.

Ocado www.ocado.com
Good for: online grocers who deliver Waitrose foods plus Daylesford Organic – superb organic butchery, cheeses, cooking ingredients, bread and wine; Natoora – burrata, rare salad leaves, vegetables including exceptional tomatoes plus cheeses from France and Italy.

Fortnum & Mason www.fortnumandmason.com
Good for: dry-aged beef (from Glenarm, N. Ireland), game, cheese, smoked salmon and many other specialities.

M & S www.marksandspencer.com
Good for: fresh, sustainably caught tuna, haddock, cod, tiger prawns and salmon; smoked salmon, poultry, game birds in season, artisan pasta including egg linguine and papardelle, 'nduja and other Italian anti pasti, Sardinian flat breads (pane carasau).

MEAT

Pipers Farm www.pipersfarm.com
Good for: exceptional meat and poultry from specialist breeds, reared to high level of animal welfare.

Thoroughly Wild Meat www.thoroughlywildmeat.co.uk
Good for: salt-marsh-reared mutton and lamb, dry-aged beef and Mangalitza pork.

Sandridge Bacon www.sandridgebacon.co.uk
Good for: raw Wiltshire cure gammons on the bone, cooked ham and bacon.

Blackface Meat www.blackface.co.uk
Good for: game, Scottish beef, lamb and mutton.

Copas www.copasturkeys.co.uk
Good for: free-range turkeys (Christmas delivery only).

Coleman's Geese* – little Hewish Farm, Milton Abbas, Blandford Forum, Dorset DT11 0DP; tel 01258 880277 email: hewishfarm@hotmail.co.uk
Good for: superb free-range geese (see image page 232) – *collect only.

Goodman's Geese www.goodmansgeese.co.uk
Good for: Free-range geese and turkeys for Christmas.

FISH

Houghton Springs fish farm – Water Lane, Blandford Forum, Dorset DT11 0PD Tel: 01258 880 058
Good for: Arctic Char, rainbow trout.

The Fish Society www.thefishsociety.co.uk
Good for: large variety of fish and shellfish, delivered frozen.

Matthew Stevens & Son www.matthewstevens-cornishfish.co.uk
Good for: Fresh fish landed by Cornish dayboats, specialising in crab and lobster.

SMOKEHOUSES

Severn & Wye Smokery www.severnandwye.co.uk
Good for: Var salmon, 'good as wild' farmed salmon from Faroe Islands, smoked Var salmon, sea trout.

Chesil Smokery www.chesilsmokery.com
Good for: smoked haddock, smoked salmon, kippers and smoked game.

DAIRY

The Fine Cheese Co. www.finecheese.co.uk
Good for: artisan cheese from Britain and Europe; biscuits for cheese.

Neal's Yard Dairy www.nealsyarddairy.co.uk
Good for: British artisan cheeses, including cheeses made by Neals Yard Creamery www.nealsyardcreamery.co.uk .

Ocado www.ocado.com
Good for: burrata; salted ricotta (from Natoora).

Waitrose www.waitrose.com
Good for: buffalo ricotta (Laverstoke Farm brand).

SPECIALITIES

The Wasabi Company www.thewasabicompany.co.uk
Good for: fresh wasabi, Japanese ingredients including roasted sesame oil, soy sauce, yuzu, ponzu.

Gourmet House www.gourmethouse.com
Good for: sustainably farmed, fairly priced caviar from Italy, Iran and China. Fresh black and white truffles in season, vegetarian 'seaweed caviar'.

Tracklements www.tracklements.co.uk
Good for: mustards, good-as-homemade pickles, chutneys, relishes and sauces.

Vallebona www.vallebona.co.uk
Good for: Italian specialist foods including procuitto, salami and all antipasti. Also cheeses and sauces.

Wai Yee Hong www.waiyeehong.com
Good for: rice-paper skins, duck pancakes, tofu and beancurd skins and hundreds of oriental cooking ingredients.

Brindisa www.brindisa.com
Good for: artisan food from Spain including cured meats, cheeses and Ortiz canned anchovies and tuna from Spain; also wood roasted peppers, beans, nuts, sherry vinegar and olive oil.

Odysea www.odysea.com
Good for: affordable Greek extra virgin olive oil, authentic feta cheese and yoghurt, beans, lentils, saffron, honey and genuine pita bread.

The Asian Cookshop www.theasiancookshop.co.uk
Good for: spices and ingredients for Indian and other Asian cooking – including masala dabba tins (clear lid spice boxes).

Bakery Bits www.bakerybits.co.uk
Good for: artisan baking equipment and ingredients including flours, yeast, essences, chocolate and sea salt.

Planet Organic www.planetorganic.com
Good for: lavash breads (thin Persian breads), unsalted pistachios, nuts, dried fruits, seeds and other natural foods.

Carluccio www.carluccio.com
Good for: pasta including egg papardelle, black olive paste, n'duja (pork and chilli paste,) truffle products.

KITCHEN EQUIPMENT

Lakeland www.lakeland.com
Good for: saucepans, kitchen knives and all gadgets, wooden boards, bowls, electrical equipment and cake or tart tins of every shape and size.

KitchenAid www.kitchenaid.com
Good for: powerful stand mixers, blenders and hand blenders, mixers and food processors.

Nisbets www.nisbets.co.uk
Good for: fast delivery of cookware, baking tins, large roasting pans for goose or turkey, storage boxes and aprons.

John Lewis www.johnlewis.com
Good for: huge range of crockery, kitchen equipment and electrical equipment for kitchens.

Knife Center www.knifecenter.com
Good for: high-quality, excellent-value kitchen knives from a USA-based specialist; an especially worthwhile source of best Japanese knives.

DISPOSABLES

JSD Products www.jsdproducts.co.uk
Good for: biodegradable, disposable party plates made of natural materials, including palm leaf plates, palm leaf spoons, bamboo skewers, authentic card noodleshop boxes with wire handles, wood crates, balsa-wood boxes, 'newsprint' greaseproof paper, wooden cones.

PARTY-EQUIPMENT HIRE SERVICES

LPM Bohemia www.lpmbohemia.com
Good for: pretty Indian tents of every size, furniture and efficient party planning. Nationwide.

Bennett's Tents www.bennetts-marquees.co.uk
Good for: lovely old -ashioned white canvas tents with wooden poles and guy ropes. Dorset only.

Vintage Rose China Hire www.vintagerose-chinahire.co.uk
Good for: china for hire from 1920s–1950s

Rayners Catering Equipment Hire www.rayners.co.uk
Good for: experienced service for hiring good-quality plain white china, glassware and cutlery – plus cooking equipment

Virginia's Vintage Hire www.virginiasvintagehire.co.uk
Good for: old tables, chairs and benches plus other furniture for parties.

INDEX

ACKNOWLEDGEMENTS

My grateful thanks to a really great team at Orion for all the passion and enthusiasm they have given to this project. The very patient Amanda Harris and editors Tamsin English and Emily Barrett, who have been wonderfully supportive, helpful and thoughtful all along. Designer Abi Hartshorne, photographer Matt Russell, assistant Nathan Sykes and food stylist-home economist Henrietta Clancy together produced truly beautiful photographs and were the best fun 'shoot companions'. Latterly, designer Clare Sivell has put together a really beautiful book. Thanks, too, to the valuable Mark McGinlay at Orion.

I also could not have done without wise, hard-working and funny Abigail Ashton Johnson on the photo shoots, or the tremendous back-up from Ralph Charlton and Alison Winn.

Great hosts have played their part, inspiring me over the years. To all of you, thank you and keep up the invitations (as I will).

Finally, to Dominic, Jack and Lara Prince, I give all my love – thank you, as always. This book is dedicated to you.

ABOUT THE AUTHOR

Rose Prince has been writing and campaigning about food for over 20 years. She writes a column for the *Telegraph Magazine* and has written four cookbooks, *The New English Kitchen* (2005), *The New English Table* (2008), *Kitchenella* (2010), which was shortlisted for a Galaxy award, and *The Pocket Bakery* (2013). In 2006 she wrote *The Savvy Shopper*, a book based on the *Telegraph* column of the same name. She also writes for the *Spectator*, the *Tablet* and is a regular contributor to BBC Radio 4's Today Programme and The Food Programme. She has won both a Glenfiddich Award and a Fortnum & Mason Food & Drink award for her food writing.

She lives in Dorset, where she runs monthly cooking courses from her kitchen.

www.roseprince.co.uk
www.roseprince-cookerycourses.co.uk

First published in Great Britain in 2017
by Seven Dials,
an imprint of the Orion Publishing Group Ltd
Carmelite House
50 Victoria Embankment
London EC4Y 0DZ
An Hachette UK Company

1 3 5 7 9 10 8 6 4 2

A CIP catalogue record for this book
is available from the British Library.

ISBN: 9780297869412
Photography: Matt Russell
Food styling: Rose Prince and Henrietta Clancy
Design and art direction: Abi Hartshorne and Clare Sivell

Printed and bound in China

The Orion Publishing Group's policy is to use papers
that are natural, renewable and recyclable and made
from wood grown in sustainable forests. The logging and
manufacturing processes are expected to conform to the
environmental regulations of the country of origin.

www.orionbooks.co.uk